GULZAR is one of  film and literary personalities of India. He is a veteran poet, lyricist, writer and director. He has written close to 1000 songs, besides writing and directing several iconic films, including *Mere Apne, Koshish, Mausam, Aandhi, Angoor, Ijaazat* and *Maachis*. He has also published books of poetry and collections of short stories—which have been translated from the original Urdu into Bengali, Marathi, Hindi, English and other languages—and a novel in English, *Two*.

NASREEN MUNNI KABIR is a reputed documentary filmmaker and writer on films. Based in London, she has made programmes on Hindi cinema for Channel 4 TV. Her several books include *Guru Dutt: A Life in Cinema*; *Talking Films* and *Talking Songs* with Javed Akhtar; *A.R. Rahman: The Spirit of Music*; *Lata Mangeshkar: In Her Own Voice*; and, most recently, *Zakir Hussain: A Life in Music*.

Jiya Jale

The Stories of Songs

GULZAR

in conversation with

Nasreen Munni Kabir

SPEAKING
TIGER

SPEAKING TIGER PUBLISHING PVT. LTD
4381/4, Ansari Road, Daryaganj
New Delhi 110002

Copyright © Gulzar and Nasreen Munni Kabir 2018

First published in hardback by Speaking Tiger 2018

All photos courtesy the authors

ISBN: 978-93-88070-97-3
eISBN: 978-93-88070-96-6

10 9 8 7 6 5 4 3 2 1

Typeset in Sabon Roman by SÜRYA, New Delhi
Printed at Sanat Printers, Kundli

INTRODUCTION

The Journey of Songs

The idea for this book dates back to 2016, when Mani Ratnam asked me to subtitle the restored print of his film *Dil Se* (1998). Subtitling dialogue can be a challenge and translating songs particularly so. There can be an infinite number of interpretations and translations of any text, but ultimately there is only one original. So when I started working on the songs from *Dil Se*, I thought it would be hugely instructive if Gulzar saab, who had written the lyrics, could guide me in conveying the essence of his words.

Gracious as ever, Gulzar saab agreed and asked me to come over the next morning to his Pali Hill home in Bandra, Mumbai. Knowing he is fabulously punctual, I made it a point to arrive on time. He greeted me warmly, asked a staff member to bring me a coffee ('Mummy-vali coffee'—this is milk coffee, no sugar—the one they make for Raakhiji) and we settled down to work in his study. We began with the iconic *Dil Se* song, 'Chal chhaiyyan chhaiyyan'. Though I had seen several English translations on the Net of this popular number, I found many very mediocre, while others seemed unashamedly comic. The best way to avoid a similar fate, I believed, was to discuss the song translations with Gulzar saab himself.

The result of this session made its way into the subtitles of the restored print of the film, and was later published in the Mumbai edition of *The Hindu* in January, 2017. The article featured the original song in romanized script accompanied by the English translation. Reading the article in *The Hindu*, it seemed such an interesting way of understanding song-writing from the point of view of the lyricist himself. Imagine how amazing it would be today to read Sahir Ludhianvi or Shailendra speak about their choice of words and images. Here was an unmissable opportunity of recording a leading lyricist of our time, Gulzar saab, and gaining an insight into his approach to song-writing.

To discuss the possibility of such a book, I went back to see Gulzar saab and fortunately he liked the idea. Straightaway he suggested contacting Ravi Singh at Speaking Tiger to ask whether he'd like to publish *Jiya Jale*. Gulzar saab added: 'Ravi is a very soft-spoken and genteel man—the perfect publisher. He talks like a poet. Let me call him.' Everything fell neatly into place, and over the next year, this book took shape.

Jiya Jale is, in fact, my second collaboration with Gulzar saab. The first being a book of conversations called *In the Company of a Poet*, published in 2012, which looked at the broader sweep of his life and work. The aim here is to focus on the backstories of how some of his most memorable songs came to be written, to discuss the work of the composers and singers with whom Gulzar saab collaborated and to translate a selection of his songs into English.

In my translations, I have avoided trying to make the lines rhyme in English, as this invariably leads to introducing new imagery into the lyrics. The translations—which have been done with the expert advice of Gulzar saab himself—are not meant to be performed, as they were not written on the metre of a tune. Rather, the idea is to help us understand the many layers beneath the lyrics. This should allow a non-Hindi or non-Urdu fan of Gulzar saab's work to get a sense of the word meanings and the spirit of the songs.

A man of many skills, Gulzar saab is a poet, film director, screenplay writer, as well as the author and translator of countless poems and books. Many of his songs have become part of the cultural fabric of Indian life; songs like 'Kajra re' are regularly played at weddings and 'Humko mann ki shakti dena' is still sung at school assemblies. His songs evoke all kinds of emotions—some political or philosophical, while others are deeply romantic. In his film songs, he combines the skills of a poet with an understanding of the demands of the narrative. Often conversational in tone, many of his songs replace a melodramatic scene or dialogue with suble suggestion. Take 'Mera kuchh saamaan…' from *Ijaazat* (1987), in which the end of a relationship is described in a heartfelt yet surprisingly matter-of-fact way. Instead of building up the drama the song words suggest a storm of inner emotions.

Many writers struggle to achieve a recognizable voice, but from his first song, 'Mora gora ang lai le' (*Bandini*, 1963), Gulzar saab's innovative style stood out. That said, some of his songs have come in for criticism over his use of metaphors. For example, critics asked how he could speak of 'the fragrance of the eyes' in 'Humne dekhi hai un aankhon ki mehekti khushboo' (*Khamoshi*, 1970). Yet it is these very unusual juxtapositions of poetic images that set him apart. We can see, when analyzing his work, that his use of imagery is not intended to be literal, but rather evocative.

Gulzar saab and I began the conversations for this book in early 2017 and they continued in stop-and-start fashion till April 2018 (I live most of the year in London, and Gulzar saab is, of course, in Mumbai). Each of our fifteen or more sessions lasted for about two and half hours and were recorded on a digital recorder, then transcribed.

Gulzar saab's sense of discipline is hugely impressive; he is at his desk, writing or reading, six days a week from 10.30 to 1.30, with an hour for lunch, before going back to his study till 6 pm. He has several books on the go at any one time and is simultaneously writing a number of songs for a number of films. Many visitors drop in and his phone rings constantly, yet his attention remained undivided when it came to our work together. He does not rest until he finds the right word and the right tone for his expression.

When the manuscript was ready, Gulzar saab and I went over it several times to get the flow right and to make sure the book accurately captured the essence of our talks.

Today there is a welcome increase in the number of books on the history of film music. This book aims to provide a novel understanding of the Indian film song. In addition, it is a behind-the-scenes record of the process of song translation from the point of view of a master songwriter who believes: 'Translation is capturing the feeling that words evoke—that's more important to me than the meaning of the words.'

NASREEN MUNNI KABIR

London

October 2018

Jiya Jale

Gulzar with Asha Bhosle and RD Burman.

Gulzar (G): Let us start with 'Jiya Jale.'

That was the first song Lataji recorded with AR Rahman. Years before working on *Dil Se*, Rahman had grown up knowing the legend of Lata Mangeshkar, and the fact that he had not recorded a single song with her prior to 'Jiya Jale' intrigued me.

One of Rahman's ways of working is thinking of a voice that would best suit his composition—and whether they are known or not, he will choose a singer whose voice matches his imagination. He's a man who is honest to his vision and for him the texture of a voice must match the tune. The singer must also be someone who is happy to go to Chennai, if they live elsewhere, and record in Rahman's studio, even if it is late into the night.

So, like a film director who has the face of an actor in his mind's eye while reading the script and understanding the nuances of a character, the face of a voice comes to Rahman. And it seemed that Lataji's face had not appeared to him before *Dil Se*. We must remember that by the mid-1990s, Rahman was *the* leading film composer in India.

Nasreen Munni Kabir (NMK): I am surprised Lataji travelled to Chennai for the recording.

G: Yes, she did. She had not met Rahman before that time, nor was she familiar with his studio, but she was willing to record there. It is not a matter of ego—these are creative artists and in creativity there is no ego. There could be a clash of egos in one's personal life but not when it comes to creating something.

As we were planning to leave for Chennai, sometime in 1997, Lataji expressed her concern to me and said it was reassuring to her that I would be there, as she knew no one at Rahman's studio. Lataji arrived in Chennai on the scheduled day and Rahman welcomed her, showing her the greatest respect, which was only natural.

Rahman has many recording studios now but for 'Jiya Jale' he decided to use the studio he first built—it had a spiritual and sentimental significance for him. When you enter the studio you see a large, imposing mixing desk. On the wall hangs a portrait of his mother and, to the side of the studio, there's a small singers' cabin equipped with microphones. An assistant who looks after the cabling kept coming in and out, but Rahman worked mostly alone that evening. Mani sir [Mani Ratnam] was there too.

Once Rahman explained the tune, we started. Lataji was led to the singers' cabin but unfortunately you could not see the mixing desk from there, nor could she see us. That was a big problem for her, as she was used to having eye contact with the composer. After one rehearsal, Lataji called me to her side: 'Gulzarji, it feels as though I am blind.'

I think she must have felt imprisoned too! Obviously we could not demolish a wall or do away with a door, so I sat on a stool outside the cabin's glass door from where I could see both Lataji and Rahman. He asked me if he should get an assistant to take my place. I reassured him it was fine by me. So that day I became the bouncing board for Lata Mangeshkar and AR Rahman. [*laughs*]

NMK: Did Lataji need many retakes?

G: No. We have a group of singers, including Lataji, Ashaji, Suresh Wadkar, Sonu Nigam and Anuradhaji [Anuradha Paudwal] who can sing a song in one go. They write the words out and mark the lyrics to indicate where they'll take a pause or add an inflection, etc. Then they are ready to record. In most other cases, the singers record their songs in sections.

Rahman records in a different kind of way. He asks the singer to sing the same line or phrase many times and keeps recording the various takes. So Lataji kept singing. Each time she sang a line, quite naturally there was a small difference in rendition—this is normal for an artist. So Rahman gives her the song, lets her make it her own, but ultimately he's the one who chooses the take he thinks works the best.

It's a totally different way of working from the old days and involves the latest technology and multi-track recording. But ultimately technology has to serve the way you like working.

NMK: Did this approach confuse Lataji?

G: Lataji knows all the alphabets of music. [*both laugh*]

Despite the fact she recorded the whole song in one session, the song itself was not finalized. Rahman then worked on it for about ten days. He usually works out the instrumentation etc., and so the song evolves slowly into its final form.

After I returned to Mumbai, he called me to discuss the 'BG' in 'Jiya Jale.' In Mumbai, we call it the interlude music—the music that comes in between the antaras [verses]—but in the South they call it BG [background].

'Gulzar saab, I have recorded a male and female chorus and inserted it in between the antaras. The words are in Malayalam, will you translate them into Hindi?'

He played the song to me over the phone. It sounded very beautiful, so I suggested we keep the chorus in Malayalam. It's the impact of the overall sound that matters. Malayalam has its own sound and folk songs have their own kind of music. Lataji and the chorus sounded wonderful. People have loved the song.

Jiya jale, jaan jale
My heart burns. My life burns

Nainon taley dhuaan chaley dhuaan chaley
Clouding my eyes, smoke rises

(Chorus in Malayalam)

Punchiri thanji konchikko
Your gentle smile delights me

Munthiri mutholi chinthikko
Kisses as sweet as grapes

Manjhani varna chunthari vaave
O sweet, lovely little girl

Thanginakka thakadhimi aadum thanka nilave
Dancing like the golden moonlight

Thanka kolusalle?
You are my golden anklets

Kurukum kuyilalle?
Like the cooing cuckoo

Maarana mayilalle?
um thanga nilave hoye
Like the dancing peacock

Jiya jale, jaan jale
My heart burns. My life burns

Nainon taley dhuaan chaley dhuaan chaley
Clouding my eyes, smoke rises

Raat bhar dhuaan chale
All night long, smoke rises

Jaanu na jaanu na jaanu na sakhi
Who knows why, O friend of mine

Jiya jale, jaan jale…
My heart burns. My life burns

Dekhte hain tann mera mann mein chubhti hai nazar
He looks at my body,
his glance pierces my heart

Hont sil jaate unke narm honton se magar
His soft lips cover my lips

Ginti rehti hoon main apni karvaton ke silsile
I keep counting the times he turns to hold me

Kya karoon kaise kahoon raat kab kaise dhale
What can I do? What can I say?
How the night passes

Jiya jale, jaan jale
My heart burns. My life burns

Nainon taley dhuaan chale dhuaan chale
Clouding my eyes, smoke rises

(Chorus in Malayalam)

Ang ang mein jalti hain dard ki chingaariyaan
Embers of desire burn inside me

Masle phoolon ki mehek mein titliyon ki kyaariyaan
Butterflies scattered in the scent of crushed flowers

Raat bhar bechaari mehndi pisti hai pairon tale
All night long my feet grind the poor henna

Kya karoon kaise kahoon raat kab kaise dhale
What can I do? What can I say?
How the night passes

Jiya jale, jaan jale...
My heart burns. My life burns

NMK: As I do not speak Malayalam, I relied on the help of a friend. I hope the translation has given us the spirit of the verse.

When we spoke of 'Jiya Jale' you once said the theme of the song is a bride's description of her 'suhaag raat' (wedding night). I must admit I didn't think this is what it was about when I first heard it. Maybe it has something to do with the fact that Mani Ratnam films it in broad daylight and in the middle of a lake!

G: Yes, but it is a kind of 'suhaag raat' song. Lataji will not sing a song that has anything to do with sex or includes vulgar words or expressions. Here there is no vulgarity at all—the night of union is a beautiful night as long you say it poetically.

Think about how Kalidas describes the features of Shakuntala—he speaks of her beauty, her lips, her breasts and figure. What makes it different is that it is poetry and by Kalidas. When describing physical beauty you do not need to be coy, but it must be done aesthetically.

You have translated 'Jiya jale', did you find anything vulgar in it?

NMK: It's sensuous but not vulgar. 'My heart burns, my life burns' is a metaphor suggesting a night of passion. I asked a friend of mine who speaks Malayalam and she said the chorus was also associated with a wedding night.

G: I did not think of a wedding night in the literal sense, though it has some vocabulary that evokes that imagery:

'masle phoolon' suggests flowers being crushed under the weight of the lovers on the bridal bed, or 'raat bhar bechaari mehndi pisti hai pairon taley' suggests the henna on the bride's feet being rubbed away. It's all in the images.

NMK: What was Mani Ratnam's brief to you? Did he tell you he wanted a wedding night song? Because the couple in *Dil Se,* played by Preity Zinta and Shah Rukh Khan, never marry and this is Preity's song.

G: It was imagining a night together when you're in love. That's why the song was not picturized as a typical wedding night. The words create the mood. I explained the meaning of the song to Mani sir and Rahman, and I remember Rahman said, 'You're a poet of images.'

NMK: Yes! It is interesting that Rahman added a chorus to a solo song.

G: A similar thing happened with the other *Dil Se* song 'Ae ajnabi.' After Udit Narayan had recorded it, Rahman telephoned me in Mumbai and said he wanted a female voice in between the antaras [verses]. He asked me for a 'pa' sounding word.

I suggested 'Paakhi paakhi pardesi.' He asked if the words had meaning or were they just sounds. I explained:

'Paakhi is Sanskrit and Bengali for bird. In Hindi it's panchhi.'

Adding the word 'pardesi' suggests it is a migratory bird. Another interpretation might suggest we're talking of a bird from a foreign land that is bound to return home one

day. Rahman recorded the line in Mahalakshmi Iyer's voice
and it sounded lovely.

I am reminded of a Hindi saying, 'Panchhi aur pardesi
nahin kisi ke meet' [Birds and strangers are not lasting
friends].

(Mahalakshmi Iyer)
Paakhi paakhi pardesi
O wandering stranger

(Udit Narayan)
Ae ajnabi tu bhi kabhi aawaaz de kahin se
O stranger, wherever you are, call out to me

Main yahaan tukdon mein jee raha hoon
I live in pieces here

Tu kahin tukdon mein jee rahi hai
You live in pieces there

Ae ajnabi tu bhi kabhi aawaaz de kahin se
O stranger, wherever you are, call out to me

Roz roz resham si hawa aate jaate kehti hai bata
The silken breeze asks as it passes each day...

Vo jo doodh dhuli masoom kali vo hai kahaan kahaan hai
...where is that pure innocent bud?
Where is she?

Vo roshni kahaan hai vo jaan si kahaan hai
Where is that glowing light?
Where is that sweet life?

Main adhoora tu adhoori jee rahi hai
I am incomplete without you.
You are incomplete without me

Ae ajnabi tu bhi kabhi aawaaz de kahin se
O stranger, wherever you are, call out to me

(Mahalakshmi Iyer)
Paakhi paakhi pardesi
O wandering stranger

(Udit Narayan)
Tu toh nahin hai lekin teri muskuraahatt hai
You are apart from me,
but your smile is here

Chehra nahin hai par teri aahatein hain
I cannot see your face,
but I hear the sound of your footsteps

Tu hai kahaan kahaan hai
Where are you?

Tera nishaan kahaan hai
Where do I find a trace of you?

Mera jahaan kahaan hai
Where has my world gone?

Main adhoora tu adhoori jee rahi hai
I am incomplete without you.
You are incomplete without me

G: I must tell you, physical distance does not exist for Rahman. When we were working with Yash Chopra on *Jab Tak Hai Jaan*, Rahman flew from LA to London, London to Chennai, Chennai to Mumbai, all within a week; all that travel so he could be in time for a music discussion with Yashji and me.

One day, out of the blue, Rahman asked me to fly to Chennai that same evening. I had to tell him:

'Look, I am not as young as you. Give me at least a day's notice, so I can sort out my work here.'

Rahman laughed. On another occasion, I happened to be in Chennai and we needed an additional song, so he said:

'You can write it here.'

'I am afraid I can't write like that. I need time.'

Then he mentioned Vairamuthu, the famous Tamil poet and lyricist:

'But he can do it. He goes into the garden and walks around. I don't know if the lyrics are hidden somewhere among the plants, but he comes back with a song!'

It must be noted that Rahman has given a new form to the film song. A good example is 'Satrangi re' from *Dil Se*. Musically it is like blank verse. There is no fixed pattern and you cannot tell when and if the mukhda [opening verse] will come again. The usual practice is the mukhda is repeated after every antara [stanza]. So when I write a song with him it's like writing a poem. The hook line may not return.

NMK: That's a major shift in the writing of a film song. I think many composers now seem to be doing a similar thing.

When it comes to the popularity of a song, do you think it's the tune or the words that first attract the listener?

G: I think it's the tune and usually a hummable tune. It's not the words. Later you want to know what the words are, so they allow you to hold onto the tune. Once you know the words then you want to know their meaning. So it goes stage by stage.

NMK: I am thinking of that catchy *Omkara* song, 'Beedi jalai le' sung by Nachiketa Chakraborty, Clinton Cerejo, Sukhwinder Singh and Sunidhi Chauhan.

G: I remember Javed Akhtar saab saying in a television interview that he liked the line 'Beedi jalai le jigar se piya, jigar maa badi aag hai' [Light your beedi with the flames of my heart, my love. A fire is raging in me] very much and wished he had written it himself. That was a sweet compliment. I think he liked it because the song has the characteristics of a folk song.

Do you remember Billo, the character Bipasha Basu plays in *Omkara*? Well, she performs the song in the film. Whenever she opens her mouth, a cuss word drops out! I took a cue from her character to develop this song. The language of *Omkara* is Awadhi and so is the song.

NMK: For those who may not know, *Omkara* is a reworking of *Othello* and is one of Vishal Bhardwaj's Shakespearean trilogies.

You must have read *Omkara*'s screenplay written by Vishal Bhardwaj, Abhishek Chaubey and Robin Bhatt?

G: One has to. I do not mean to point fingers at anyone but most songwriters today ask about the situation or the location—will the song be filmed outdoors or indoors, is it a solo or a duet? But it's the script that guides you to write a song that works with the narrative. You must also match the song's vocabulary with the speech of the characters.

Three characters in the scene sing 'Beedi jalai le'. The points of view shift between Kesu [Vivek Oberoi], Billo [Bipasha Basu] and Langda Tyagi [Saif Ali Khan]. The first verse is from Kesu's point of view. He talks about not having a quilt or cover and it's freezing cold, so he's tempted to snuggle under his neighbour's quilt.

(Sukhwinder Singh)
Na gilaaf, na lihaaf
No cover, no quilt

Na gilaaf, na lihaaf, thandi hawa bhi khilaaf, sasuri
No cover, no quilt.
This wretched wind blows against me

Itni sardi hai kisi ka lihaaf lai le
It's so cold that you want to slip
under someone's warm quilt

Jaa padosi ke chulhe se aag lai le
Go, take the embers from your
neighbour's fireside

Sunidhi Chauhan sings for Billo and her point of view takes over—here she suggests that her lover light his beedi with passion. I could have said, 'Light your cigarette,' but that did not sound very poetic. So I used 'beedi'—it gave the song a flavour of the village and the small town. Billo warns Kesu not to blow smoke out of his mouth when he leaves her house because prying eyes might see the smoke— implying gossip will spread.

(Sunidhi Chauhan)
Beedi jalai le jigar se piya
Light your beedi with the flames
of my heart, my love

Jigar maa badi aag hai
A fire is raging in me

Dhuaan na nikaari o lab se piya
Don't let the smoke escape your lips,
my love

Yeh duniya badi ghaagh hai
This world is full of prying scoundrels

(The song then switches back to Kesu.)

Na kasoor, na fatoor
Not my fault, not my folly

Na kasoor, na fatoor, bina juram ke hazoor mar gaye
Not my fault, not my folly.
Punished without committing a crime

Here Billo takes over again and describes how badly the all-powerful zamindar treats her and forces her to dance and entertain his friends in the zamindar's court [kachehri].

Aise ek din dupeheri bulai liyo re
He summoned me on an afternoon like this

Baandh ghungroo kachehri lagai liyo re
Tied dancing bells to my ankles,
turning his court into a dance hall

…bulai liyo re, dupeheri
Yes, he summoned me

(Sunidhi Chauhan & Sukhwinder Singh)
Angeetthi jalai le jigar se piya
Light the coal stove with the flames
of my heart, my love

Jigar maa badi aag hai
A fire is raging in me

Then we return to the feudal context. Kesu and Langda sing this verse together. It's a description of the personality and behaviour of the cruel and powerful zamindar.

(Sukhwinder Singh, Nachiketa Chakraborty &
Clinton Cerejo)
Na toh chakkuon ki dhaar
No knife is as sharp

Na daraanti, na kattaar
No sickle, no dagger

Aisa kaate ke daant ka nisaan chhod de
It's his sharp teeth that leave deep marks

Ye kataai toh koi bhi kisaan chhod de
No farmer is ready to cut his crops

Aise jaalim ka chhod de makaan chhod de, Billo
Stop living in the house of such a tyrant,
sweetheart

(The last verse is Billo's and describes the night her
sweetheart came to see her.)

(Sunidhi Chauhan)
Na bulaaya, na bataaya
No message, no warning

Hume neend se jagaaya, hai re
Waking me from deep sleep

Aisa chaunke lihaaf mein naseeb aa gaya
I was taken aback to find my lover
under my quilt

Voh elaichi khilai ke qareeb aa gaya
Sweetening my mouth with a cardamom,
he snuggled up

Koyla jalai le jigar se piya
Light the coal with the flames
of my heart, my love

Jigar maa badi aag hai
There's a raging fire in me

NMK: Wow! That's a story within a song!

G: Language is my profession and if my profession was engraving names on utensils, how could I master language?

NMK: That's true!

Now, I have a rather naive question to ask. I hear this word 'sasuri' occasionally in dialogue and in some of your songs like 'Beedi jalai le.' Can you tell me something about it?

G: It's a colloquial word, literally meaning 'mother-in-law.' 'Sasura' is father-in-law. It is not a gaali. I don't know the origin of the usage—in UP it's commonly used, not only when talking about men and women, but you can even say:

'Ye bakri kaaboo mein nahin aati, sasuri, pata nahin doodh kaise degi' [This goat, this sasuri, can't be controlled, who knows how it will give milk?].

In Hindi, you would not say: 'My sasuri said...' You'd say 'Meri saas, or meri saasu ne kaha' [My mother-in-law said]. 'Sasur' is a very respectful term for father-in-law. So you might say 'sasuri' is a figure of speech.

NMK: It has an interesting and nice sound.

G: And it's affectionate.

NMK: Your song 'Dil toh bachcha hai' from the 2010 film *Ishqiya* is very moving. You wrote it for Khalujaan, the character played by Naseeruddin Shah, a lovable rogue who is considered beyond the age of falling in love.

With great ease you waltz in words like 'haaji,' 'peeri'

and 'wallah.' These words describe Khalujaan's personality and his cultural background effortlessly.

Aisi uljhi nazar unse hatt ti nahi
So entangled was our gaze,
my eyes could not turn away

Daant se reshmi dor katt ti nahi
Teeth cannot cut the threads of love

Umr kab ki baras ke safaid ho gayi
Years have showered down on me,
now turning white

Kaari badri jawaani ki chhatt ti nahi
The dark clouds of youth refuse to pass

Walla ye dhadkan badhne lagi hai
But oh, how the heart quickens

Chehre ki rangat udne lagi hai
The blush from my face fades

Darr lagta hai tanha sone mein ji
Sleeping alone frightens me

Dil toh bachcha hai ji
The heart is a child

Thoda kachcha hai ji
A little unripe

Haan dil toh bachcha hai ji
Yes, the heart is a child

Naseeruddin Shah and Vidya Balan in Abhishek Chaubey's
Ishqiya (2010).

Kisko pata tha pehlu mein rakha
Who knew the heart I had by my side…

Dil aisa paaji bhi hoga
…would turn out to be so unruly?

Hum toh hamesha samajhte thhe koi
I always believed it was…

Hum jaisa haaji hi hoga
…as pious a creature as me

Haye zor kare, kitna shor kare
How insistent it is, what a fuss it makes

Bewaja baaton pe ainvey ghaur kare
Reading meaning into the meaningless

Dil sa koi kameena nahin
No one is as wicked as the heart

Koi toh rokey koi toh tokey
*Someone must stop it,
someone must scold it*

Is umr mein ab khaaoge dhokhe
At this age it will only be cheated

Darr lagta hai ishq karne mein ji
Falling in love frightens me

Dil toh bachcha hai ji
The heart is a child

NMK: How did this song come to you?

G: The idea has to come from the script. Khalujaan has fallen in love with a young girl and he's old. Everyone calls him 'Chacha-jaan' [dear uncle]; even the girl he has a crush on calls him 'uncle.' But love happens. So how does Khalujaan justify it? He says it's his heart that's a child and has childish ways.

Besides I could not write a romantic song like 'Your flowing hair and your eyes have enchanted me.' Something like that would not go with Khalujaan nor suit his age.

NMK: So the heart never ages? It never grows up?

G: It never grows up is a negative expression; the heart stays young is a positive expression. That's the difference. There is always an innocent child in your heart who wants love and needs love. I am in the same age bracket as Khalujaan and I could easily fall in love with a young girl—but it is Naseeruddin Shah who falls in love in my place. [*both laugh*]

NMK: Rahat Fateh Ali Khan brings such a gentle tone to the way he sings 'Dil toh bachcha hai.' What is he like as a person?

G: Shall I call him Rahatji, Rahat bhai? Rahat saab? He's a very dear person. 'Khush dil, khush mizaaj' [having a cheerful temperament] is the best way to describe him. He's a most unassuming man.

Rahat Bhai has sung other songs I've written but the

memorable thing about this song is that Vishal and I recorded it in Lahore at Rahat Bhai's farmhouse, where he has built a recording studio. We arrived in the evening only to see him greeting us wearing a pair of shorts. Wearing shorts goes against the image one has of a celebrated singer of romantic songs, so I immediately took a photo and joked that I would show it to everyone in Mumbai: 'Look, he wears shorts when recording a love song!'

Rahat Bhai's diction is unique. It has a Punjabi flavour—a flavour he shared with his celebrated uncle, the late Nusrat Fateh Ali Khan saab. There's a line in the song: 'Umr kab ki baras ke safaid ho gayi.' Rahat Bhai does not say 'safaid,' which is the usual way of pronouncing the word. He says 'sfed'… It sounds so endearing and gives the song a casual, intimate feel.

Aisi udaasi baitthi hai dil pe
Heavy is the sadness that weighs
on my heart

Hasne se ghabra rahe hain
Now even laughing makes me feel uneasy

Saari jawaani katra ke kaatti
I spent my youth staying clear of love…

Peeri mein ttakra gaye hain
… only to confront it in old age

Dil dhadakta hai toh aise lagta hai vo…
When my heart beats fast I sense…

Aa raha hai yahin dekhta hi na ho
... love is sneaking up on me

Prem ki maare kattaar re
Stabbing at my heart

Taubah ye lamhe katt te nahi kyun
O God, why do these moments not pass?

Aankhon se meri hatt te nahi kyun
Why do they not leave my sight?

Darr lagta hai khudse kehne mein ji
Admitting I'm in love frightens me

Dil toh bachcha hai ji...
The heart is a child

G: Rahat Bhai sang another song in *Omkara*, 'Naina tthag lenge.' Only Vishal can understand phrases like these—the eyes make promises that are not legally binding. I find it an interesting way of describing the eyes.

Nainon ki jubaan pe bharosa nahin aata
Do not trust the promises of eyes

Likhat padat na raseed na khata
No receipt, no ledger entry

The choice of words has a folk song flavour, which is also present in Vishal's tune and in Rahat saab's voice and diction. These combinations just happen—they cannot be designed. The way Nusrat Ali Khan saab sang or the way

Rahat saab sings—you can't design that diction. It's an in-born talent and that is where Rahat saab stands out.

Nainon ki mat maaniyon re, nainon ki mat suniyo
Do not heed the eyes. Do not listen to them

Nainon ki mat suniyo re, naina tthag lenge
Do not heed the eyes. They'll only deceive you

Jagte jaadu phoonkenge re jagte jagte jaadu
Wide awake, you'll fall under their spell

Jagte jaadu phoonkenge re neendein banjar kar denge
They will rob you of all sleep

Bhala manda dekhein na paraya na saga re
The eyes do not tell good from bad,
loved ones from strangers

Nainon ko toh dasne ka chaska laga re
The eyes take pleasure in stinging

Nainon ka zeher nasheela re
Their poison makes you drunk

NMK: In December 2016, I went to the launch of *Nude*, Vishal Bhardwaj's book of poetry. During the panel discussion Vishal laughingly said:

'My poems feel like pirated versions of Gulzar saab's poetry.'

He went on to talk about how you encouraged him to write poetry. Why did you push him in that direction?

G: Vishal is like a son to me. You feel good about your children. [*laughs*]

We met over twenty years ago, when he was as young as he is today. Vishal is full of energy and always ready to experiment. He understands poetry extremely well and is very sensitive to it. When we work together on a song, he often comes up with a word. Even if it is not exactly the word that works, I can see he is on the right track. His suggestions are poetic. I encouraged Vishal to publish his poetry so that it would not be lost. He should not remain a casual poet. Once his book is published, he becomes an author—sahib-e-kitaab.

Vishal's father, Ram Bhardwaj, was a poet and wrote songs in the films of the 1970s and 1980s. Vishal's elder brother, who has now passed away, was a film producer. So the world of films is not alien to Vishal and, because his father wrote lyrics, the connection to poetry came naturally to him.

By the way, Vishal must have fifty or a hundred mukhdas [opening lines] that I have written. Some were for songs that were put aside or intended for films that were shelved. There are times when we have revisited these mukhdas. Vishal would pick out three words, for example, 'Namak ishq ka' and say:

'Can you make a mukhda on these words?'

Vishal is an unusual man in that he'll reject his own tune if it does not suit a film or if he feels he could do better. I have not seen this trait in anyone else. Once a music director has composed a song, even if it is not quite right, he/she will modify it, but essentially, they will not reject it completely. Vishal will discard a tune outright: 'No, it is not working, let me try something else.'

For me, it means I have to write fresh lyrics for the new tune and find another way of looking at the same narrative situation.

At one time, the maximum number of songs I had written were with Pancham [RD Burman], but now I think that record has been broken by my work with Vishal.

NMK: How would you describe his music?

G: Vishal does not stick to one musical form. In Bengal they have the Sanchari. It's a form of poetry that does not come straight from mukhda to antara—which is the pattern the film song has traditionally followed—mukhda to antara. Only Vishal understands the form of the Sanchari well and uses it often in his compositions.

NMK: I read a good translation of Sanchari on the Internet—'wandering.' It seems to accurately describe the form you're talking about.

Could you give me an example of the Sanchari as used by Vishal?

G: 'Namak ishq ka.'

NMK: Could I translate 'Namak ishq ka' as 'the spice of love?' The salt of love is too literal.

With Vishal Bhardwaj.

G: Yes, that's right, 'spice' is what is meant. The first line 'Main chaand nigal gayi' [I swallowed the moon] is in fact the title of a book of mine.

NMK: Before we discuss the song, I was keen to know why a doha [couplet] precedes the main song?

G: The doha allows you a glimpse of the song's theme. You set up the punchline but do not reveal it. You present the words and the ambience. 'Main chaand nigal gayi, O daiya re daiya [I swallowed the moon, O pity me],' and then finally you come to—'laaga re laaga, namak ishq ka' [My tongue touched the spice of love]. So the punchline is the mukhda.

NMK: Is it like the 'alaap'?

G: Yes. In the alaap, the musician first presents the notes of the raga he or she will perform—'hum jisse arohi-avarohi kehte hain ya vadi-samvadi' [We call them the ascending and descending notes of a raga].

You prepare the audience, you make them familiar with the raga by playing these notes and you create an atmosphere—a classical singer might also throw in a song line in the alaap like 'Prem ki maare kattaar.' That's a raga sung by Bade Ghulam Ali Khan saab. The singer will work around that line and elaborate upon it. And the second line is the punchline. Sometimes the first line can also be the punchline, it depends on the form.

[*Reading the song lines*] In 'Namak ishq ka,' you have the line 'Bheetar bheetar aag jare' [A fire burns within]—'jare' is 'jale.' In folk, 'la' becomes 'ra.' 'Jabaan pe laaga, laaga re namak ishq ka'—my tongue has touched the spice of love.

The song continues with 'Tez tha tadka ka karun'— 'tadka' is the seasoning you add to daal to spice it up. 'Si-si karti'—'si-si' is a kind of gasping sound one makes when you taste a hot chilli. You pull in your breath. When translating this line try 'Si-si, I gasped.' For 'baniye' keep 'grocer' in the singular. That way you individualize him.

The meaning of 'Raat bhar chhaana chhaana re namak ishq ka' is 'using a sieve to find the spice of love among other spices.'

Main chaand nigal gayi daiyya re
I swallowed the moon, O pity me

Bheetar bheetar aag jare
My throat was on fire

Baat karun toh senkh lage
I feel the heat rise when I speak

Main chaand nigal gayi daiyya re
I swallowed the moon, O pity me

Ang pe aise chhaale pade
My body is covered with blisters

Tez tha jhonka ka karun
The seasoning was hot

Sisi-sisi karti main marun
'Si-si' I gasped

Jabaan pe laaga laaga re
My tongue touched...

Namak ishq ka
... the spice of love

Haaye tere ishq ka
Your love

Balam se maanga maanga re
I asked my beloved for...

Namak ishq ka
... the spice of love

Haaye tere ishq ka
For your love

Sabhi chhede hain mujhko, sipahiye baanke chhamiye
Everyone teases me—policemen, thieves and loafers

Udhaari dene lage hain gali ke baniye-vaniye
Even the local grocer offers me credit

Koi toh kaudi tu bhi lutta de
Why don't you spend some money on me?

Thodi thodi shehed chatta de, thodi thodi
Why not taste a little honey?

Tez tha tadka ka karun
The seasoning was hot

Sisi-sisi karti main marun
'Si-si,' I gasped

Raat bhar chhaana re chhaana re
All night long I looked among the spices…

Namak ishq ka
… for the spice of love

G: Rekha Bhardwaj and Rakesh Pandit have sung this song. Rekha is unlike all other singers. I remember she had to struggle in the early days. She's a disciple of the classical singer Pandit Amarnath Mishra and her training in classical singing is solid, so it's easy for her to sing folk.

In the beginning some people in the film industry felt Rekha's voice was a little too different. Now they realize that that difference is her strength. People have to be true to themselves. They should not follow in the footsteps of others.

Rekha has a kind of 'roohaaniyat' [spiritual/soulful quality] in her voice, which is why the Sufi songs that feature in my non-film album *Ishqa Ishqa* [released in August 2005] come alive through her singing. She can be playful too.

NMK: Her voice can sound flirtatious but she never sounds vulgar.

G: Exactly, because her voice has that spiritual quality. In 'Teri raza, meri raza,' you feel she's immersed in the song.

NMK: We can capitalize 'you,' so the translation will read 'Your wish,' for 'Teri raza,' etc. This will make it clear the song is addressed to God.

Teri raza, meri raza
Your wish is my wish

Tu hi mera qaazi
You decide all

Pehle bhi tu, aage bhi tu
It began with You. The future is You

Tu hi mera maazi
My past is You

Beet rahi hai, teri dua hai
I live thanks to Your blessings

G: 'Teri dua hai, teri raza hai'—it's Your blessings, it's Your wish. 'Dua' is in the previous line.

Sajde bichhaaye hain dar pe tere
I have bowed at Your threshold

Tu hi hai kya kaabe mein
Is it You in the sacred Kaaba?

Sachchi bata
Tell me the truth

Teri raza ...

Na kadam dikhe na nishaan pada
I saw no footstep or trace of You

Ik gubaar utth ke utar gaya
Just a haze drifted by

Main qareeb hi thha khada hua
I was standing near

Mere paas se tu guzar gaya
I could feel You pass me

G: You will find many references to God in my poetry—I do not deny Him but I do not accept Him. I question Him and ask why He does not appear before me.

I'll give you the gist of another poem of mine that speaks of God. God and I are passing each other on either side of the road. I know He sent me signals, but He never looked into my eyes. Now keeping us apart is the traffic of religions—so I start doubting—'are You looking for me or are You hiding from me?'

NMK: Do you believe in God?

G: I don't believe in a God who keeps tabs on your life. He is not an accountant [*laughs*]. So it depends on your definition of God. I believe there is a force, a system of the universe or universes.

NMK: You mean a life force?

G: You can give it whatever name you want. 'God' is one of those names. In 'Teri raza, meri raza' you have another kind of dialogue with God. There is faith, intensity and questioning.

Sunta raha sehta raha tere intezaar mein
I listened, I endured as I waited for You

Aaya na tu sadiyaan hui, chashm-e-ashakbaar mein
You have not appeared for centuries
in my teary eyes

NMK: If I could go back to 'Namak ishq ka,' we have discussed how it begins with a doha—do you like the use of the doha—having introductory lines to a song?

G: Yes, but it has become something of a cliché. It was less frequently used in the days of, say, SD Burman. The song would come straight from the opening music to the first line of the lyrics. If you study the early songs, they usually start with opening music and not words.

NMK: I found an example of a Shakeel Badayuni song composed by Naushad Ali for the 1951 film *Deedar*. The song opens with a doha, written by Muztar Khairabadi, Javed Akhtar's grandfather. Mohammed Rafi has sung it so beautifully:

Asir-e-panja-e ahd-e-shabaab kar ke mujhe
Kahaan gaya mera bachpan kharaab kar ke mujhe

Imprisoning me in the claws of intoxicating youth
Having undone my life, where has my childhood flown?

Then Shakeel Badayuni's lyrics follow—'Huey hum jinke liye barbaad' [The one who has destroyed me].

G: But you can see the connection in theme between Muztar saab's doha and Shakeel saab's song, otherwise it would not have worked.

Similar to the prelude in a novel, the doha is a kind of a song prelude. 'Kahaan gaya mera bachpan kharaab kar ke mujhe' is followed by 'Huey hum jinke liye barbaad voh humko chahe karein na yaad ...' [Where has my childhood flown? The one who no longer remembers me has destroyed my life ...]

Shakeel Badayuni saab is continuing the thought that you find in Muztar saab's doha. But it is usually the same lyricist who writes the doha and the song itself. Most music composers and film directors ask for a doha because they prefer not to start with opening music. They need something from where to build the song, so they like the idea of words doing that, and then the punchline follows. I personally find this is overused now.

NMK: But it does set up a dramatic entry for the tune. When you say this form is overused, does it feel tired to you?

G: It's not in my hands. It's up to the music directors. I tell them it's overused. Shankar Mahadevan has become conscious of this repetition and admits: 'The last four songs I have sung have a doha at the start. People have stopped introducing the song with the music.'

Salilda [Salil Chowdhury] once asked me to write a doha for the song 'Ganga aaye kahan se, ganga jaaye kahan re' [From where does the Ganges flow? To where does the Ganges flow] from *Kabuliwala*. It was based on a Bengali tune. I remember Rajinder Krishan was sitting in the music room with us while we were working. Rajinder Krishan turned to Salida and suggested:

'Why not use the mukhda of "Ganga aaye kahan se..." as an opening doha?'

His idea saved me because I could not think of anything right then and there that would serve the purpose. So in the final song you have Hemant Kumar singing the first lines in a doha style:

Ganga aaye kahaan se, Ganga jaaye kahaan re
Aaye kahaan se, jaaye kahaan re
From where does the Ganges come?
To where does it flow?

Leharaaye paani mein jaise dhoop chhaaon re
Like sunlight and shade dancing on the waves

Raat kaari din ujiyaaraa mil gaye donon saaye
Where night and twilight meet

Saanjh ne dekho rang roop ke kaise bhed mitaaye re
See how the dusk has united form and colour

Leharaaye paani mein jaise dhoop chhaaon re
Like sunlight and shade dancing on the waves

NMK: How lovely to have one lyricist suggest something to another and that becomes the final song. Then there is Hemant Kumar's haunting voice.

G: Hemantda's voice reminds one of a Baul singer. When I hear him—that's the image that comes to me—a Baul singer sitting by the river and singing. The sound echoes, spreads over the water and fills the sky. That's how I would describe Hemantda's voice.

He was also the only singer I knew who, while recording a song at the mike, would light a cigarette and keep it in an ashtray near him. Imagine that! He was a regular smoker and smoked Marlboros. He did not worry about looking after his throat. He would take a drag during the musical interludes of the song. I asked him about it and he said it made the grain in his voice sound natural. That's Hemant Kumar—a tall man in every way. It was a pleasure working with him.

NMK: How much of a team member are you when you write songs for a film?

G: You cannot be an outsider in the filmmaking process. You are a member of the team. You have to play your part, even if you must rewrite the song ten times. I have done that. Sometimes I get fed up, especially if the director keeps asking for more options. We're not cooking chhole bhature. Songwriting is a serious thing.

NMK: What about the playback singers? How involved are they in the whole process?

G: Lataji and Ashaji have always asked the age of the character they were singing for—which is so rare. I haven't been asked this question by any other singer.

NMK: You can see why their voices worked so seamlessly with the stars they lent their voices to.

Did Kishore Kumar not ask you about the kind of character he was singing for?

G: No, I don't remember if he did. Rafi saab would ask me to give him details about the song situation and who the actor singing it on screen was—so he would modulate his voice according to whether he were singing for Johnny Walker or Rajendra Kumar. That's a perfect and complete playback singer for you.

NMK: Do you think the way Hindi and Urdu film songs have been sung has in some way evened out the many accents of Hindi—made them homogeneous? For example, can one identify a regional accent in a song?

G: You can hear regional flavours. For example, Lataji and Bhupenda [Bhupen Hazarika] each recorded their version of 'Dil hoom hoom kare' for Kalpana Lajmi's *Rudaali*. If you hear both versions of this song, you'll recognize the difference in tone. Assamese folk music has been soaked up by Bhupenda's voice and you hear it in the way he says 'hoom hoom.'

Dil hoom hoom kare, ghabraaye
When my heart quickens, it makes me uneasy

Ghan dham dham kare, darr jaaye
When the clouds roar, it frightens me

Ek boond kabhi paani ki mori akhiyon se barsaaye
If only a teardrop would fall from my eyes

G: The 'when' is important in the first two lines—keep them in your translation.

NMK: We have talked about how a film song must be seen in the context of the narrative. Can we take this particular song and see how it works with the story?

G: 'Rudali' is a short story written by the famous Bengali writer Mahasweta Devi. The film is based on her story. Since I wrote the screenplay and dialogue, I knew the nuances of the language.

Rudaali is set in Rajasthan and centres around Shanichari [Dimple Kapadia], a low caste woman, a Dalit, who becomes a professional mourner—a 'rudaali'. They are women who are hired to weep at funerals of the upper castes because it is seen as below the status of the family to show emotion. So the line: 'Ek boond kabhi paani ki...' describes Shanichari's troubled heart; despite being a 'rudaali' she is unable to shed tears over her own plight. The main line—dil hoom hoom kare—refers to the uneasiness in her heart.

> Teri jhori daaroon, sab sookhe paat jo aaye
> *If I filled your lap with dry leaves...*

> Tera chhua laage, meri sookhi daar hariyaaye
> *... your touch would turn them green*

These lines are about Shanichari's relationship with Lakshman Singh, the young landlord [Raj Babbar], and are expressions of her feelings for him—feelings he returns.

The dry leaves are symbolic of her sadness, and if she gave them to him, he could ease her sorrow.

The next verse refers to her repressed feelings for the landlord. Shanichari is achhut [of the Untouchable caste] and though Lakshman has touched her in the desert on the day he accepted water from her hands, they both know he should not have touched her at all. So 'Jis tann ko chhua tu ne...' refers to that scene.

> Jis tann ko chhua tu ne, us tann ko chhupaaoon
> *I hide the body you once touched*

> Jis mann ko laage naina, voh kis ko dikhaaoon
> *To whom can I show the heart you once saw?*

> O morey chandrama, teri chaandni ang jalaaye
> *O moon of mine, your moonlight burns my body*

> Teri oonchi attaari maine pankh liye katvaaye
> *With clipped wings,*
> *how can I fly to your high abode?*

> Dil hoom hoom kare, ghabraaye
> *When my heart quickens, it makes me uneasy*

G: 'Teri oonchi attaari' is an allusion to Lakshman Singh's status and high caste. How can she ever be equal to him? In the film, Shanichari sings this song in the presence of Lakshman Singh and his father [Amjad Khan]. Lakshman understands the subtext of the words.

I believe when people write about film songs they must know the language well and, more importantly, they should know how films are made. Work on a film in some capacity and it will give you an idea of the filmmaking process. Writing as an outsider does not provide the complete story.

NMK: Your situating 'Dil hoom hoom' within the narrative is most helpful in making the connection between song and narrative.

That said, this song works equally well outside of the film context. It has, as we know, a male and female version. What were the challenges you faced when switching gender?

G: Two versions were required because of the story, though we were not repeating the same narrative situation. When writing two versions, I had to change some lines to match the other situation and be alert to gender. Sometimes the composer even changes the tune—to give the song a little variation.

NMK: When a composer sings his own composition, in this case Bhupen Hazarika singing 'Dil hoom hoom kare,' is this an advantage?

G: It's a very big advantage because he's the creator of the song. A composer knows the delicate nuances of the notes he has used. That's why the songs of Salil Chowdhury, SD or RD Burman and Bhupen Hazarika cannot be rendered a hundred per cent as they conceived them. Even the most excellent singers interpret the song in their own way. There is always a slight variance. It is only natural for a singer, say Ashaji, to make the song her own. The song will have traits of her personality. After all, songs are not sung by computers [*laughs*].

The temperament of creative people—whether singer, painter, composer—is always reflected in their work. When you hear a Salil Chowdhury song, you know it is Salil Chowdhury's music. Reading your writing, your translations and subtitles, people who know your work will recognize Nasreen Kabir's style. They can tell by your choice of words.

So the choice of words in my songs is bound to be different from other lyricists. Javed Akhtar once said to me:

'When I hear a song, I can tell from the very first line
that the song has been written by you.'

It is a great compliment because I know it is difficult to achieve a recognizable voice. Javed saab is a poet and a very good songwriter, so his words meant something to me. I have read his poetry and I also know when Javed saab's pen is behind this or that song. For example, he likes similes. I can also identify the songs of Indeevar, Hasrat Jaipuri and Shakeel Badayuni. You see their hand at work through their choice of words.

NMK: You have translated many poems into Hindi/Urdu and recently you even translated your novel *Two* into English. Can you tell me how you approach translating a poem as opposed to a song?

G: When translating a poem, I am not bound to any image. I will translate it according to the feeling that the poet has stirred in me. It won't be the literal meaning of the words. The translation will depend more on the theme of a poem. For a film song, the translation has to stay close to the words because these relate to the images on screen and to the story.

NMK: People sometimes try to make a poem or a song rhyme in translation to match the original. I am not too fond of this. But is this a good idea?

G: Rhyming limits you. It becomes a handicap. You have to force words into the translation that don't always work. Basic poetry started from there. When poetry grew up, it became free verse. The meaning and the thought behind a poem are more important than the need to justify a rhyme.

In poetry there is blank verse and free verse. And there are poems called prose poems—known as 'nasri nazm' in Urdu. These poems have no metre, whereas blank verse and free verse have metre.

Personally, I prefer to stick to metre because the rendering is better. At least you get the rhythm of poetry. But it's a matter of personal choice. At the end of the day, writing is not a compulsion—it is a profession and a craft.

NMK: Craft? Or inspiration?

G: Craft, more than inspiration. One should master the profession one practices.

NMK: I have asked many composers about what music has given them. So I ask, what has poetry given you?

G: It's the means by which I express what I feel—feelings first, thoughts second.

NMK: And the individual's feelings are present in their work?

G: Yes. Anyone who tries to sing like Rafi saab or Lataji has never become them. For that matter, has anyone achieved the success of our great playback singers, including Mukeshji, Ashaji, Kishore Kumar or Geeta Dutt? Find your own voice, your own expression.

By the way, did you know Rafi saab appeared in a film?

NMK: Yes, in the 1947 film *Jugnu* with Dilip Kumar. Rafi saab appears in one scene singing, 'Voh apni yaad dilaane ko ek ishq ki duniya chhod gaye, jaldi mein lipstick bhool gaye, rumaal puraana chhod gaye' [She left me a world of love to remind me of her, in her hurry she forgot her lipstick and an old handkerchief]. It was something like that! An unusually modern concept, I could imagine these lines being written today.

G: That's true.

NMK: When I look at your style of writing, I see you often juxtapose a description of an abstract feeling with something real and concrete. I'm thinking of your book title, 'Chauras Raat' [The Square Night]. You give the night an abstract shape, which provides a fresh touch.

Perhaps these unusual pairings are the key to recognizing Gulzar saab's voice.

G: It is not something I do consciously. 'Daanista jisse kehete hain ...' [doing something unconsciously]. It's not deliberate ...

NMK: Your distinctive voice is in all your songs. It takes a different turn in 'Chal chhaiyyan chhaiyyan'. I find this a particularly unique song from every angle. Your lyrics, Mani Ratnam's direction, Rahman's music, Santosh Sivan's photography, Farah Khan's choreography, the performance by Shah Rukh Khan and Malaika Arora, the voices of Sukhwinder Singh and Sapna Awasthi, and not forgetting the train chugging through lush Ooty—you have all conspired to make this a truly memorable piece of cinema.

G: When Shah Rukh heard the song, he fell in love with it. I am guessing that the words 'chhaiyyan chhaiyyaan' made them think of a chugging train [*both laugh*].

NMK: I believe after Shailendra's 'Mera joota hai Japaani' in Raj Kapoor's *Shree 420*, 'Chhaiyyan chhaiyyan' is now *the* Indian film song that is recognized the world over—millions know it as 'the train song'. Sir Andrew Lloyd Webber once said in an interview that he had seen the *Dil Se* song clip on Channel 4 TV in the UK and it made him want to work with Rahman, which led to the production of the musical *Bombay Dreams* in London. The song even popped up under the opening credits in Spike Lee's 2006 film *Inside Man*.

I remember seeing *Inside Man* on its release in Toronto, and when the song was heard at the start of the film, two young women wearing hijaabs jumped out of their seats and screamed 'Shah Rukh Khan!' You can imagine the reaction of the Canadian audience, who fell very silent [*both laugh*].

I must admit it is a difficult song to translate and am grateful for your help. I remember reading a translation on the Net of the first line: 'Come, let us walk under the shadow, shadow, shadow, shadow.' That's a lot of shadows to deal with!

G: Actually it is not 'shadow', it should be 'shade'!

Jinke sar ho ishq ki chhaaon
Those who walk in the shade of love...

Paaon ke neeche jannat hogi
... must have paradise beneath their feet

Jinke sar ho ishq ki chhaaon
Those who walk in the shade of love...

Chal chhaiyyan chhaiyyan chhaiyyan chhaiyyan
Come, let us walk in the shade of love

Sar-e-ishq ki chhaaon chal chhaiyyan chhaiyyan
Let us walk in the shade of love

Paaon jannat chale chal chhaiyyan chhaiyyan
Let paradise spread beneath your feet

Chal chhaiyyan chhaiyyan chhaiyyan chhaiyyan
Let us walk in the shade of love

Voh yaar hai jo khushboo ki tarah, jis ki zubaan Urdu ki tarah
The beloved friend is like a sweet aroma
whose words as elegant as Urdu

Meri shaam raat meri kaayenaat
My evening, my night, my universe…

Voh yaar mera sainyyan sainyyan
…that friend of mine is my beloved

Chal chhaiyyan chhaiyyan chhaiyyan chhaiyyan
Let us walk in the shade of love

NMK: I was struggling with the 'gulposh' line—it was the most difficult line in the song. But you explained it by telling me that 'posh' means attire or dressed in flowers, referring to God. I hope this works?

Gulposh kabhi itraaye kahin
meheke toh nazar aa jaaye kahin
The One draped in flowers will come into sight
as the fragrance spreads

Taaveez bana ke pehenoon usse
aayat ki tarah mil jaaye kahin
I shall wear an amulet, if the beloved
is found in holy verse

Voh yaar hai jo imaan ki tarah
My beloved is like faith itself

Mera naghma vohi, mera kalma vohi
My song, my prayer

Yaar misaal-e-uos chaley, paaon ke taley firdaus chaley
The beloved falls like dew,
paradise beneath the feet

Kabhi daal daal kabhi paat paat
Sometimes on the branches,
sometimes on the leaves

Main hawa pe dhoondoon uske nishaan
I search for traces of my beloved in the breeze

Sar-e-ishq ki chhaaon chal chhaiyyan chhaiyyan
Let us walk in the shade of love

Paaon jannat chale chal chhaiyyan chhaiyyan
Let paradise spread beneath your feet

Chal chhaiyyan chhaiyyan chhaiyyan chhaiyyan
Let us walk in the shade of love...

Main uske roop ka shehdaai
I am an admirer of the beloved's lovely form

Voh dhoop chhaaon sa harjaai
Voh shokh hai rang badalta hai
Fickle as the sun and shade.
Changing colour on a whim

Main rang-roop ka saudaai
I am enchanted by colour and form

Jinke sar ho ishq ki chhaaon
Those who walk in the shade of love...

Paaon ke neeche jannat hogi
... must have paradise beneath their feet

Meri shaam raat meri kaayenaat
My evening, my night, my universe...

Chal chhaiyyan chhaiyyan chaiyyan chaiyyan...

NMK: I was talking to Zakir Hussain about the line 'Gulposh kabhi itraaye kahin meheke toh nazar aa jaaye kahin,' and he asked whether you were thinking of a dargah of a Sufi saint—because a shrine is often covered with flowers.

G: The lines can suggest a dargah. But the idea here is that God is hidden among the flowers—gulposh literally means 'He has worn flowers'. You can use abstract imagery when speaking of spirituality.

NMK: So draped in flowers is all right?

G: Yes, and so when the fragrance spreads then I know where God is hidden.

NMK: If I understand correctly, many of your songs talk of the 'experience of feeling,' rather than being a description of events.

G: [*pauses*] Absolutely right.

I am not trying to give a simile or paint an image—I want to create an experience of feeling. And what is that feeling? I might be fumbling to catch an image—that fumbling itself becomes the expression.

NMK: Could you give me an example of an older song where you evoke the experience of feeling through abstract imagery?

G: Take the song 'Humne Dekhi Hai Un Aankhon Ki Mehekti Khushboo' [I have seen the fragrance of your eyes]. Saying 'fragrant eyes' is what makes the song abstract.

Let me give you an example of a Jagjit Singh song—'Tere Khayaal Ki Aabu-Hawa Mein Jeete Hain' [I live in the world of your thoughts]. Now 'aabu-hawa' means environment, but if you separate aab and hawa, individually the two words mean water and wind. Saying, 'I live in the water and wind of your thoughts' is absurd. So it is not the literal meaning of the words that one must seek.

When I talk of the fragrance of the eyes, it is not physical. Eyes do not use words but they can express anger, hatred and love—there is a tone and flavour in the way they speak. So could you not imagine a fragrance when you see soft, loving eyes? That said, I faced a lot of criticism when it came to this song. 'How can he see the fragrance of eyes?'

NMK: It's such a haunting song and Lataji's singing and Hemant Kumar's tune make it sublime. It's also the abstract imagery that makes it stand out.

For the translation of the lines 'Pyaar koi bol nahin, pyaar awaaz nahin,' 'Awaaz' could be either 'voice' or 'sound.' Which is it for you?

G: 'Love is not words, love is not a voice.' Use 'voice' instead of sound.

NMK: 'Na ye bujhti hai na rukti hai na ttheheri hai kahin'.

G: The flame cannot be extinguished.

NMK: Can I go for 'snuffed out'? Sounds a bit Shakespearean!

G: Why not? Keep it!

NMK: For 'muskuraahat si khili rehti hai aankhon mein kahin,' can I go with 'flowing like a smile in your eyes?'

G: That's an interesting expression. Fine.

NMK: 'Hont kuchh kehete nahin kaanpte honton pe magar.' 'The lips never part to speak yet they quiver so.'

G: Beautiful line. Now read the whole translation to me.

Humne dekhi hai un aankhon ki mehekti khushboo
I have seen the fragrance of your eyes

Haath se chhu ke isse rishton ka ilzaam na do
Do not taint it with the burden of relationship

Sirf ehsaas hai ye rooh se mehsoos karo
It's just a feeling, feel it with your soul

Pyaar ko pyaar hi rehene do koi naam na do
Let love be love, do not burden it with a name

Humne dekhi hai …

Pyaar koi bol nahin pyaar awaaz nahin
Love is not words. Love is not a voice

Ek khaamoshi hai sunti hai kahaa karti hai
It's a silence that speaks, a silence that hears

Na ye bujhti hai na rukti hai na ttheheri hai kahin
It cannot be snuffed out,
stopped or stilled

Noor ki boond hai sadiyon se bahaa karti hai
It is a droplet of radiant light that falls eternally

Sirf ehsaas hai ye rooh se mehsoos karo
It's only a feeling, feel it with your soul

Pyaar ko pyaar hi rehene do koi naam na do
Let love be love, do not burden it with a name

Humne dekhi hai…

Muskuraahat si khili rehti hai aankhon mein kahin
Flowering like a smile in your eyes

Aur palkon pe ujaale se jhuke rehete hain
Glowing on your lowered eyelids

Hont kuchh kehete nahin kaanpte honton pe magar
Lips never part to speak yet they quiver

Kitne khaamosh se afsaane rukey rehete hain
So many silent tales frozen in time

Sirf ehsaas hai ye rooh se mehsoos karo
It's only a feeling, feel it with your soul

Pyaar ko pyaar hi rehene do koi naam na do
Let love be love, do not burden it with a name

Humne dekhi hai…

NMK: You once told me Hemant Kumar was supposed to sing this song, not Lata Mangeshkar. Is that right?

G: Yes. But Hemantda refused:

> 'No, Lata is the only one who can sing this composition. I can't sing it. Lata will sing.'

I protested:

> 'Dada, how is that possible? The song is written from a man's point of view. How can the heroine talk about her lover in these terms? It is such a feminine image. Have you ever met a man whose eyes exude a fragrance?' [*laughs*]

I have always said Lataji can change the gender of a song and till now no one has questioned why a male singer did not sing this song. That's Lata.

NMK: When she read the lyrics, did she find the idea of fragrant eyes an odd expression?

G: No. She didn't say anything and neither did Hemantda because he understood poetry and was among the great exponents of Tagore's songs. He understood metaphors. It was the critics who took objection to the concept.

> 'Is this some kind of new poetry? Where is the poetry in this? Does it mean you can write anything you like?'

NMK: I wonder how you feel about your song translations on the Net. A lot of people enthusiastically translate your songs all the time. Some translations are good, some are just awful and many are comic.

G: Let them carry on. Why should I stop them? I really don't have the time to sit and translate my songs for everyone. So they come up with their own understanding of the lyrics.

NMK: I believe there are some people who write poems and sign your name on the Net and on Facebook. Is this true?

G: Why only Facebook? These poems show up on the mobile. WhatsApp is full of them. Sometimes these fake poems are forwarded to me. A friend reads a poem somewhere and sends it to me, even congratulating me.

There are other friends who find these fake poems when browsing the Net and they email them to me. Ninety per cent of the time these poems are not mine. I find it deeply hurtful. They create this fake poetry by picking some words from a poem of mine and then they start knitting their own poem together—the kind of poem I do not count as poetry at all. They're so badly written. All I request is—please sign your own name and don't make me the plagiarist.

My friend, Salim Arif, has started a Facebook page in which he prints my original poems—a poem for each day. He calls the page, 'Don't go by the look, go buy the book.'

NMK: That's a clever pun [*both laugh*].

G: Salim Arif believes the people responsible for this fake poetry have heard of my poems but haven't read them. But if they have not read my poems, how do they take words

With Lata Mangeshkar and RD Burman.

or lines from them? They should quote the source. Instead they carry on writing bad poetry in my name.

One day two girls came to my gate and left a poem and a cake with my watchman. The cake was to celebrate a poem that had completed a year on WhatsApp! That poem was not even mine.

NMK: How did you react to this strange situation?

G: I sent the poem to Pavan Jha who looks after the Facebook page and my website—gulzaronline.com. Now when he comes across a fake poem, he writes under it NBG—'Not by Gulzar.'

By the way, when Pavan Jha put the poem that the two girls had left for me on the Facebook page, a lady got in touch with him saying that she had written that poem, though it was credited to Gulzar saab. As a result she had not been recognized for having written it. When Pavan asked her why she had not protested, she explained:

'The reaction of people on the Internet is too aggressive. Besides, the poem has been forwarded from one person to another hundreds of times. What can I do?'

NMK: This new world of communication has brought out a lot of intellectual dishonesty. I agree, it's an insult to your work.

G: There's no sense of shame. If someone is trying to become a poet, however weak their poetry may be—start from scratch but make it your own. Don't copy or discredit others. Because of the simple language I use, people believe anyone can write. So why not try it?

NMK: Your simple language is not so simple, as we are discovering while translating! The point is, they don't see how your voice shines through your work.

It's like you writing a poem and signing Ghalib. I know you would never dream of doing such a thing.

G: If I were to write a rubbishy poem under the name of Ghalib and if people appreciated it, it means they have never read Ghalib. In the same way, if they read a poem that was not written by me and think it is mine, then they do not know my work.

I once wrote a poem, 'Aadatein bhi ajeeb hoti hain' [Habits are strange things], and someone made it 'Auratein bhi ajeeb hoti hain' [Women can be strange].

NMK: That's outrageous.

G: Absolutely.

NMK: Despite this irritating and somewhat uncontrollable situation, I know you believe that poetry must be open to interpretation.

G: It has to be, otherwise it would not have survived. Scholars would not still be working on Ghalib's poetry if his verse had only one meaning. Take Shakespeare—there are thousands of scholars all around the world analyzing his plays and sonnets, and that's after 400 years.

Poetry is like a diamond. From different angles it reflects different colours and shapes.

A master of Urdu poetry, Dr Bashir Badr, once recounted an amusing story. As a young man, he had to analyze his own verse for an exam paper. The examiner read Badr saab's paper and said:

'This is not the meaning of this couplet.'

'Sir, it is I who have written it.'

'No, no, this is not the meaning of the couplet—*this* is what it means…'

The examiner refused to accept Dr Bashir Badr's interpretation, even though it was Badr saab who had written the couplet [*both laugh*].

NMK: If we look at the rich history of Hindi film music, what is a perfect song for you?

G: I would give the example of Sahir Ludhianvi's song, 'Mann re tu kaahe na dheer dhare' [O heart of mine, learn to be patient].

This song was written for Kidar Sharma's 1964 film *Chitralekha,* which happened to be a remake of the director's own film of the same name. The 1941 film was with Mehtab and Nandrekar.

Roshan composed 'Mann re' and Mohammed Rafi saab sang it so brilliantly. It is the perfect example of a perfect lyric. Sahir saab usually wrote in Urdu or Hindustani. Here he has used Hindi, perhaps not as well as masters like Pandit Narendra Sharma, but his usage is far superior to many.

The song suits the character, the narrative situation and the language of the film's dialogue. I place that song on a very high pedestal. It's so beautiful.

NMK: It's exquisite, philosophical and thoughtful.

G: Yes, it is also lyrical. The words flow effortlessly and are not moralizing or lecturing.

NMK: Adding 're' to 'mann' creates, I think, a certain intimacy. A softening.

G: It adds a folk flavour too. 'Kaahe' is Awadhi, while 'dheer dhare' is classical Hindi. So Sahir saab is mixing words and traditions and associations of language. Plus it is sung like a poem.

There is the other Sahir saab song in *Jaal*...

NMK: 'Yeh raat yeh chaandni phir kahaan?'

G: Yes. That's another beautiful song.

The other lyricist I've spoken about many times is Shailendra, whom I consider the best lyricist in Hindi cinema. He has blessed cinema with his work.

Instead of talking directly about romance in *Parakh*, we have this lovely girl in a village strolling along the banks of a river, and as she picks up a flower, she sings 'Mila hai kissi ka jhumka' [I have found an earring that belongs to someone]. Bimal Roy's picturization is so special. Although the word 'jhumka' means earring, she is describing the shape of the flower that resembles an earring.

The other *Parakh* song 'O sajana, barkha bahaar aayi'

is also very beautiful, but I especially like 'Mila hai kissi ka jhumka, hare bhare neem taley'. What a lovely simple way to describe nature—'beneath the green tree lies this flower'.

NMK: You often talk about DN Madhok. What makes his songs exceptional for you?

G: DN Madhok was a pioneer.

When songs came into Indian films in 1931, they came from the stage. The work of Agha Hashr Kashmiri, the Urdu Parsee theatre, the ghazal, the classical bandish, Urdu poetry, mythology and bhajans—these were the principal influences on the early film song. DN Madhok's first film was *Radhe Shyam* in 1932 and, when he started writing songs, he introduced a different dialect and rich folk imagery.

Think of DN Madhok's *Rattan* song, composed by Naushad Ali, 'Jab tum hi chaley pardes lagaa kar tthes, o preetam pyaara, duniya mein kaun humaara' [When you went away, it was a blow to my heart, O sweet beloved, who can I now call my own in this world?]. All the *Rattan* songs were big hits.

NMK: I remember 'Akhiyaan mila ke jiya bharmaake chaley nahin jaana' [Don't make me fall in love with you, then break my heart and go away]. He also wrote the famous K.L. Saigal song 'Diya jalaao' in the 1943 film *Tansen*.

G: DN Madhok changed the vocabulary of the film song. He was regarded among the first generation of films lyricists along with Kavi Pradeep and Kidar Sharma. Madhok saab also wrote screenplays and directed many films from the 1930s to the 1950s.

Kidar Sharma brought influences from the Urdu ghazal, nazm and folk. He wrote many songs on the 'panchhi' [Birds/flight of birds]. There is no logic as to why he did that—I think it's just choosing a certain imagery to represent thoughts and ideas. He spoke about birds and I keep using the image of the moon. I find so many ways of talking about the moon.

Think of Shailendra's beautiful line: 'Dum bhar jo udhar mooh pherey, O chanda, main unse pyaar kar loungi.' Imagine telling the moon to turn his face away—what a line! Hats off to Shailendra. That's what a poet can do.

NMK: You were close friends with the fantastic Shailendra. Did you discuss his film songs with him?

G: We knew each other well but he was my senior after all. We talked about poetry and contemporary literature, but not about film songs. Shailendraji was a man of literature and was involved in the trade unions. Many of his poems show his commitment to leftist ideology.

As you know he was the person who pushed me into writing songs in the first place. Today that song is a landmark in film music. When I wrote 'Mora gora ang' for *Bandini*, I used an unusual metaphor. We had read lines like: 'Rahu chaand ko nigal gaya' [an eclipse has swallowed the moon], but as far as I know no one had scolded the moon in poetry:

'Tohe raahu laage bairi, muskaaye jee jalai ke' [May you be eclipsed for smiling at my suffering, O moon].

Bimalda [Bimal Roy] and Sachinda [SD Burman] appreciated this new approach.

NMK: We know the leading names in songwriting, but what about the lesser known lyricists?

G: Among the old stalwarts were Pandit Narendra Sharma, Bharat Vyas and Neeraj. They brought the colour of Hindi into their songs. For the past two decades the language of the song has become somewhat stuck between Punjabi and Urdu.

Today's lyricists write well too. Amitabh Bhattacharya, Irshad Kamil, Swanand Kirkire. Prasoon Joshi stands out with a new voice—he brought back the kind of beautiful Hindi that Pandit Sharma or Bharat Vyas would use. Prasoon can recite his poetry on stage very well.

I would compare Swanand Kirkire to the old master songwriter DN Madhok. Swanand has that kind of diction. He uses language from the folk tradition, which is rarely heard now. Both Prasoon Joshi and Swanand Kirkire are not only writers, but they are also singers. And their parents are classical singers.

NMK: I cannot think of many past women lyricists, but we have Kausar Munir today.

G: Kausar Munir comes from a family of learned writers. That is why her language has a literary diction and she expresses herself very effectively.

NMK: You speak of the current generation of lyricists; how do you find time to listen to their songs?

G: The entire pattern of time has changed with the changed pace of life. In the old days we had only Vividh Bharati and Ameen Sayaniji's 'Binaca Geetmala' and his 'Fauji Bhaaiyyon ka Programme'.

We used to listen regularly to these very popular radio programmes. People would look forward to them and many would send in their 'farmaish' [request letters]. All day long we would hear certain names repeatedly on the radio—Lata Mangeshkar, Mohammed Rafi, Shankar-Jaikishan, Shailendra, Hasrat Jaipuri and others. Rajinder Krishan and Shailendra were the lyricists' names we heard most frequently until Anand Bakshi took over.

Now I hear film music thanks to my friend and tennis partner, Umesh Pachigar. He picks me up from the house at 6 am to go to the Bandra Gymkhana, where we play tennis. He is my Vividh Bharati now. The radio is on and we listen to Hindi film songs on the way to the Gymkhana and back.

Umesh is an architect and a keen ballroom dancer. When we hear the old songs, he immediately identifies the beat and says:

'This is a Cha-Cha-Cha, this is a Foxtrot and that's a Samba. But when I hear the songs today, I can't identify the beat. I only feel like beating my head against the wall!'

And Umesh and I have a hearty laugh. So much has changed with technology. Almost a revolution in communications came with the mobile phone. Now there are more than a hundred radio stations and a vast number of TV channels in India broadcasting around the clock. There is no time for a song to have a full impact. The pace of life and music has become so fast and loud that the words have taken a back seat. So have the lyricists.

It is so unfortunate that there are no TV channels dedicated to classical music or to our rich tradition of folk music which exists in all the different Indian languages.

NMK: It is well known how Shailendra persuaded you to write your first song for Bimal Roy. You have always praised this splendid filmmaker. Even though there is so much written about this first song of yours, and how it changed the course of your life, we must include it here.

> Mora gora ang lai le, mohe shyaam rang dai de
> *Take away my fair skin,*
> *make me dark-skinned like Krishna*

> Chhup jaaungi raat hi mein, mohe pi ka sang dai de
> *I shall hide into the dark night,*
> *bring my beloved to me*

> Mora gora ang lai le ...

> Ik laaj rokey paiyyan ik moh kheenche baiyyan
> *Shyness holds my feet back,*
> *feelings tug at my arm*

> Jaaun kidhar na jaanu humka koi batai de
> *Which way shall I turn? Will someone tell me?*

Mora gora ang lai le …

Badari hatta ke chanda, chupke se jhaanke chanda
Parting the clouds, the moon steals a look at me

Tohe raahu laage bairi, muskaaye jee jalai ke
May an eclipse swallow you!
You smile at my suffering, O envious moon

Mora gora ang lai le …

Kuchh kho diya hai pai ke, kuchh paa liya ganwaayi ke
I lost something only to find something

Kahaan le chala hai manwa mohe baavari banai ke
Where is my heart taking me,
having turned my head?

Mora gora ang lai le …

NMK: From your very first song we can see you like using 'lai le' rather than 'ley le' or 'jalai le,' rather than 'jala le.'

G: The moment you say 'Mora gora ang lai le,' you know it's Awadhi. It is how people speak in north Indian villages. And so you know the character singing this song in the film is someone living in a village or a small town, just by the vocabulary. Once you use Awadhi, the whole song has to be written in Awadhi. 'Mora' is not 'mera,' and 'lai le' is not 'ley le.'

NMK: You write the words for a song, then work with the composer, the song is recorded and finally there's the picturization—that's when you see your words come alive on the screen. And each director/choreographer has yet another interpretation of the song—to make it work visually. Let us take the example of Mani Ratnam. Do you like his approach to song picturisation?

G: It's absolutely superb. When I saw his *Raavan*—I can still say I have never seen such visuals in an Indian film. You can see the painter in his framing, composition and movement. As one frame changes to the next, you feel a fluid camera at work. There is never a dull frame in his movies.

NMK: You wrote a very unusual song 'Tthok de killi' for *Raavan.* What was that song all about?

G: Mani sir was clear about the political slant of the character Raavan, played by Abhishek Bachchan. Raavan is a Dalit and his people are oppressed, so they fight back. When we have a rebel, a Robin Hood type, we can ask ourselves why this character has evolved into the person he has become and what's the reason behind his actions? Robin Hood is Robin Hood because of the injustices of the king.

In the same way, Raavan and his people come together because of the injustices of the rulers. When Mani sir explained the context of the song, I thought of it as a Dalit anthem.

Tthok de killi O tthok de killi
Hammer in the nail!

Ke door nahin hai, chalega Dilli
It's not far, you coming to Delhi?

Sab ko ghoore aankh dikhaaye, taanashaai kare-karaaye
The authoritarian glares at all,
threatening and fearsome

O bagad billi O tthok di killi
O wild cat, hammer in the nail

Tu maar de danda uda de gilli
Use your stick, let the gilli fly

NMK: This line refers to the amateur rural sport gilli-danda, played with two sticks. The large stick [danda] is used to hit the smaller stick [gilli] as far as it can go.

Where does this expression 'tthok de killi' come from?
G: The Punjabi lines are 'Chakde phatte, tthok de killi, ajj jalandhar teh kal dilli.' Navjot Singh Sidhu made these lines popular.

The lines were a freedom fighter's cry against the British. 'Lift the planks [chakde phatte], hammer in the nail [tthok de killi], ajj jalandar teh kal dilli [today Jalandhar, tomorrow Delhi].' It has the spirit of a war cry. 'Tomorrow we're challenging the authority in Delhi!' So that's where the phrase comes from.

NMK: Fascinating origins—even more so when you know the song's background. How do you think listeners read a song?

G: They probably think of the surface meaning of the words. And then some may look for layers of meaning below the surface. Words cast shadows and lines have dimensions. The more you scrape the surface, the more you'll find. You will discover 'Tthok de killi' is not an individual's point of view, instead it tries to express the raw energy of a whole community.

NMK: I would like us to talk about language and the power of words. Hindi and Urdu are sister languages and both have great beauty, but what is it about Urdu that makes it so special for you?

G: I believe every language has its own character. Sanskritized Hindi is very beautiful. The shloks are so musical. Bengali is very sweet. You must remember that the script of Devanagri is the most scientific script in the world—what you speak is what you write.

For me, Urdu has a royal presence and an aristocratic diction. There is a line in a poem of mine relating to this, would you like to add it here?

'Faqiri mein nawaabi ka mazaa deti hai Urdu [Urdu makes the poor feel like royalty].'

NMK: Lovely!

G: You asked why Urdu is special to me? It starts with my personal experiences and feelings. I studied it at school in Delhi. After the Partition, people started learning Hindi and there was a lot of prejudice against Urdu. It is sad that anyone could be prejudiced against this language. Urdu phonetics are special and, when used in combination with Hindi, it beautifies the Hindustani we speak.

We must not forget that Urdu is an Indian language. It has evolved from many Indian dialects and languages such as Awadhi, Bhojpuri and Purbi. Some phonetic sounds in Urdu like *t, tth, d, dd* do not exist in any other language—not in Arabic or Persian. But these sounds are to be found in Indian languages.

NMK: I believe 'pa' does not exist in Arabic.

G: That's right. In Urdu, *bh, ph, tha* and *dha* have come from Sanskrit—and bhai, bhabhi, bhojan, dhakkan, etc.

NMK: Given your love of Urdu, no wonder you wrote 'Jiski zubaan urdu ki tarah' in the famous 'Chhaiyyan Chhaiyyan'. There are many who quote this line now.

G: 'Chhaiyyan' is actually 'Hindustani', not pure Urdu. The word 'chhaiyyan' means 'chhaaon' ['shade' in Hindi]. In Hindi poetry we say: 'Bansuri baaj rahi kadam ki chhaiyya.' This is a reference to Lord Krishna playing the flute under the shade of the Kadam tree [step tree].

The majority of film songs are in fact written in Hindustani. They have shades of both Urdu and Hindi. That is their strength and beauty. Gandhiji once said to stop calling it Urdu or Hindi and call the national language 'Hindustani'. That way we could avoid confusion and prejudice.

NMK: Can we look at 'Voh shaam kuchh ajeeb thi' from the 1970 film *Khamoshi*? It is so romantic and has a beautiful melody. Few composers besides Hemant Kumar could have created such a haunting tune and Kishore Kumar sings it so beautifully.

Voh shaam kuchh ajeeb thi, yeh shaam bhi ajeeb hai
That evening was strange,
this evening seems strange too

Voh kal bhi paas paas thi, voh aaj bhi qareeb hai
She was close to me yesterday,
she feels near me today

Voh shaam kuchh ajeeb thi…

Jhuki hui nigaah mein kahin mera khayaal tha
Her eyes were lowered,
but she was thinking of me

Dabi dabi hansi mein ik haseen sa gulaal tha
A lovely pink glowed in her half smile

Main sochta thha mera naam gunguna rahi hai voh
I thought she was humming my name

Na jaane kyun laga mujhe ke muskura rahi hai voh
I don't know why it seemed to me
she had a smile on her face

Voh shaam kuchh ajeeb thi…

Mera khayaal hai abhi jhuki hui nigaah mein
Thoughts of me still linger in her lowered eyes

WAHEEDA REHMAN
RAJESH KHANNA

ख़ामोशी

Gitanjali's

KHAMOSHI

DIRECTED BY ASIT SEN · PRODUCED BY HEMANT KUMAR

Khili hui hansi bhi hai dabi hui si chaah mein
In her carefree laughter, in her unspoken desire

Main jaanta hoon mera naam gunguna rahi hai voh
I know she is humming my name

Yahi khayaal hai mujhe ke saath aa rahi hai voh
I keep thinking she'll soon be walking by my side

NMK: Songs today don't seem to have this kind of romanticism.

G: Romance has changed, romantic attitudes have changed and so has language. Culture is not static, it has to change and with it everything changes over time—your clothes, your food, your behaviour, your music and your way of romancing.

Many years ago, when our films were shown overseas, they used to cut out the songs and make the films 90 minutes long. Audiences abroad were not keen on our songs but now it is our songs and dances that attract them.

The attitude to our cinema in the West has changed. There were master film composers in earlier times, though they were not appreciated abroad. But Rahman has done it. He won two Oscars in 2009 for *Slumdog Millionaire* and his name appeared again in the Oscars' longlist in 2016. He has taken Indian film music to an international audience.

NMK: I remember you told me you did not attend the Oscar ceremony to collect your award for Best Lyrics for 'Jai Ho' because you didn't have a black jacket.

G: That's right [*both laugh*].

NMK: 'Jai Ho' is a song full of vigour.

G: It's a masterpiece by Rahman. I must also give credit to Sukhwinder Singh because his voice brought a lot of energy to it. He should have got more mileage from the popularity of that song. He contributed enormously to it. Sukhwinder is steeped in folk music and works very hard. When he talks to you, he keeps slipping into song.

NMK: The words of 'Jai Ho' are terrific too. I love the idea of a 'silver-threaded sky'. It has unusual imagery.

> Aaja aaja jind-e shaamiyaane ke taley
> *Come, come under the canopy of life*
>
> Aaja zariwaale neele aasmaan ke taley
> *Come under the silver-threaded sky*
>
> Jai ho, jai ho…
> *Hail Victory!*
>
> Ratti ratti sachchi maine jaan gavaayi hai
> *I spent every moment of my life…*
>
> Nach nach koylon pe raat bitaayi hai
> *… dancing on burning coals*
>
> Akhiyon ki neend maine phoonkon se uda di
> *I blew away the sleep from my eyes*
>
> Gin gin taare maine ungli jalaayi hai
> *Singed my finger pointing at the stars in the sky*

Aaja aaja jind-e shaamiyane ke taley
Come, come under the tent of life

Aaja zariwaale neele aasmaan ke taley
Come under the silver-threaded sky

Jai ho
Hail victory!

NMK: Was Danny Boyle at the song recording?

G: No, there was only Rahman and Sukhwinder. 'Jai Ho' worked well in the film. It's a story about a young boy and girl who fall in love and after overcoming many obstacles, they come together. It is not a Noor Jahan and Jehangir story. Do you understand the love affairs of this generation?

NMK: Somewhat! I think people are freer to stay and freer to leave a relationship if it's not working.

Your song 'Mera kuchh saamaan' from the 1987 film *Ijaazat* could be called a break-up song today.

G: Pancham used to call it my luggage song [*laughs*]. He found it very funny. He would ask me to read the lines to him:

Mera kuchh saamaan tumhaare paas pada hai
Saawan ke kuchh bheege bheege din rakhe hain
Aur mere ik khat mein lipti raat padi hai
[Some of my things are lying with you.
A few rainy days of the monsoon in an envelope.
And a night wrapped in a letter I wrote]

The song describes a relationship that's ending. I have used very concrete images—like rainy days, a letter and the night—and made them abstract by adding words like 'bheegey bheegey din' [rainy days] or the idea of 'mere ik khat mein liptti raat padi hai' [And a night wrapped in my letter]. You don't fold rainy days in an envelope or wrap a night in a letter.

The other words, 'Geela mann shaayad bistar ke paas pada ho' [There's a moist heart near the bed]. What does this imagery suggest? A heavy heart and tears shed on the pillow.

Mera kuchh saamaan tumhaare paas pada hai
Some of my things are lying with you

Saawan ke kuchh bheege bheege din rakhe hain
A few wet monsoon days...

Aur mere ik khat mein liptti raat padi hai
... and a night wrapped in my letter

Voh raat bujha do, mera voh saamaan lautta do
Snuff out that night. Send my things back to me

Patjhad hain kuchh, hai na?
It's autumn, isn't it?

Patjhad mein kuchh patton ki girne ki aahat
The sighing of a few falling autumn leaves...

Kaanon mein ik baar pehen ke lautta aayi thi
... were worn as earrings when I left

Patjhad ki voh shaakh abhi tak kaanp rahi hai
That autumn branch still trembles

Voh shaakh gira do, mera vo saamaan lautta do
Cut off that branch. Send my things back to me

Ek akeli chhatri mein jab aadhe aadhe bheeg rahe the
Under a lonely umbrella, we were getting half wet

Aadhe sookhe aadhe geele sookha toh main le aayi thi
Half dry, half wet. I took the dryness with me

Geela mann shaayad bistar ke paas pada ho
You'll perhaps find a tearful heart near the bed perhaps

Voh bhijwa do mera voh saamaan lautta do
Send that to me. Send my things back to me

Ek sau sola chand ki raatein, ek tumhari kaandhe ka til
One hundred and sixteen moonlit nights,
the mole on your shoulder

Geeli mehendi ki khusboo, jhoott-moott ke shikve kuchh
The aroma of wet henna,
a few make-believe complaints

Jhoott-moott ke vaade bhi sab yaad kara do
Remind me what were those
make-believe promises

Sab bhijva do, mera voh saamaan lautta do
Send everything to me.
Send my things back to me

> Ek ijaazat de do bas jab is ko dafnaaungi
> *When I bury those things, allow me…*
>
> Main bhi vahin so jaaungi
> *… to sleep close to them*

NMK: Can I translate the last line as 'bury those memories'? Instead of bury those things?

G [*pauses*]: Yes, 'memories' is good.

> Ek ijaazat de do bas jab is ko dafnaaungi
> *When I bury those memories, allow me…*
>
> Main bhi vahin so jaaungi
> *… to sleep close to them*

NMK: You said that RD Burman would call this your luggage song. When it became such a humungous hit, did it surprise him?

G: While we were recording the song, he said he had changed his mind about it. At first he thought it was too long. But when Ashaji started humming a line, he started enjoying it. It did not matter if the song was a hit or not. Pancham knew it was a good composition…something new, something different.

Whenever Ashaji performs on the stage, she tells me the audience always requests her to sing this song.

NMK: 'Mera kuchh saamaan' received the National Award for Best Playback Singer and Best Lyrics in 1988. It really does describe heartbreak in a fresh way.

The song is also in nearly every favourite Gulzar playlist. Most people can identify with it because the emotions associated with breaking up are common experiences.

Are these images from an imaginary or lived experience?

G [*irritated*]: It's in front of you, so how can it be imagination? You have to be involved. That's the job of a writer or a poet. You can't remain aloof and unconcerned when writing a poem or a song.

NMK: And what if it is not your lived experience? Someone may not have lived a romantic life yet write romantic songs.

G: We come to the sensitivity of a poet. How much does he empathize with the suffering of people? Or imbibe the pains of society? A poet tries to understand the human condition.

NMK: And feel compassion?

G: More than compassion. A poet must find the words that express all kinds of emotions, whether he experiences something directly or indirectly.

NMK: I am reminded of what Javed Akhtar once said to me:

> 'A journalist has to witness a moonlit night to report it, while a poet can imagine a moonlit night in the middle of the day and write about it.' [*both laugh*]

I am curious to know if the approach you take when writing lyrics for a film which you're directing is different from writing lyrics for another director?

Rekha and Naseeruddin Shah in a still from *Ijaazat* (1987).

G: I have written all the songs in my films. When I write the script, there is no difficulty in working the song into the story. Take 'Mera kuchh saamaan.' I don't think anybody would have thought of having a similar song in that narrative situation. While I was writing the *Ijaazat* screenplay, it came to me like a poem.

As I was picturizing the song, I knew I did not want it to be filmed in one location. I wanted to cut between indoor shots/the present time, and outdoor shots/the flashbacks. I had an excellent cameraman, Ashok Mehta, and together we discussed the images I had in mind and which were evoked by the words—I needed a shot of the couple walking in the rain—their umbrella is nearly blown away by a strong gust of wind.

NMK: In India, the credit for a song is divided between choregrapher, director, composer, lyricist, singer and finally, the actor who brings it alive on the screen. For the most part, popular singers in the West write their own songs and music.

G: Are you thinking of Bob Dylan, who won the Nobel Prize for literature? Yes, he's a good example of someone who combines all these talents. In India, the situation is different, especially when it comes to film music.

NMK: How do you see the relationship between composer and lyricist?

G: It's a two-way relationship. If we see it from the composer's point of view—he's curious about how the lyricist will react to his tune and what thoughts and images it will suggest to the songwriter. Will I describe a cloudy day or a starry night on his melody?

And if you write the words first, you ask yourself what kind of tune your words will inspire in the composer.

NMK: When you wrote 'Dil dhoondta hai' [The heart searches...] for *Mausam*, you once explained how you had expanded on Ghalib's poem, imagining the different situations that the heart seeks.

The gifted Madan Mohan composed this song. What do you remember about working with him?

G: I remember how he used to conduct his orchestra. The session musicians who worked with him made it a point to come on time for his recordings. But there were always some habitual latecomers. He would look at them as they entered the recording studio and say, 'Khaala ka ghar hai? Come...' [You take this for your aunt's house?]

He'd tell them to sit down but not play. That was the punishment. If need be, he would change the orchestration but he would not let the latecomers play—it was his way of saying he could do without them.

Madanji would conduct the orchestra from behind a big glass partition at Famous, Tardeo. He would move his arms about, lifting the baton etc., then sometimes his eyes would fall onto his well-toned arm muscles and he would look at them proudly! [*both laugh*]

He was a very well-built, strong man and used to wear tight, half-sleeved T-shirts. He had great style and was very handsome. I used to wonder sometimes if he had come to Mumbai to become a star.

NMK: His son Sanjeev Kohli has a lot of style too. He's always punctual, super-efficient and very talented. He reworked and presented his father's music in *Veer-Zaara* so beautifully.

G: That's right.

NMK: Was working with Madan Mohan easy?

G: Easy? I don't know how to put it. He would sing a tune to me, and some days later when he sang that same tune, it was different. He used to keep improvising with the result, so I would have to change a line, take out a word or add one. Madanji's compositions were always changing.

The first couplet of 'Ji dhoondta hai phir vohi fursat ke raat din' is by Ghalib. I developed the song from Ghalib's line. While Madanji was working on the composition, he changed 'ji' to 'dil.' I objected:

'Madanji, you can change my words, but not Ghalib's. We can't take that liberty with Ghalib.'

He didn't say anything and we continued rehearsing at sound recordist Minoo Kartik's studio at Famous.

The next day, Madanji brought his copy of 'Diwan-e Ghalib' to the studio:

'Gulzar saab, I kept quiet yesterday because I wanted to check something first.'

In the edition of 'Diwan-e Ghalib' that Madanji owned, the word at the start of the couplet was 'dil.' And in my edition it was 'ji.' Both editions were authentic. It was also known that Ghalib himself would change words. When we finally came to recording the song, Madanji asked me to keep 'dil' because it ended with a 'l,' and that created a resonating sound like 'dhaa' on the tabla. I liked the idea.

So the song is 'Dil dhoondta hai.' Personally, I preferred the slower version, though many composers preferred the faster version because they say it is very difficult to compose on that 'taal' [rhythm/beat].

NMK: Madan Mohan was famous for his ghazal compositions. Why was that?

G: Because he knew poetry well. He knew the mizaaj [temperament] of the ghazal. He used to read Urdu poetry. And that was true of Jaidev too. All composers who know Urdu poetry understand the temperament of the ghazal.

NMK: Was there anything unexpected that you've observed about the personalities of the music composers with whom you have worked?

G: I noticed how much they enjoyed cooking—we'll talk later about my watching Ustaad Allarakha saab cook for us in America!

I'd like to first talk about how fascinating it was to watch Madan Mohanji in the kitchen. He would hold a glass of whisky in one hand and, with the other hand, he stirred some mutton in a pan. He hummed a tune throughout the stirring and frying—*ti ti tee*...that's the sound he made when he was humming. And if the mutton curry needed a bit of water, because it had started to stick to the bottom of the pan—in went his whisky! [*both laugh*]

He was a terrific cook and cooked with great style. He would keep singing while telling me that Lataji was on her way for rehearsal. He had a music room in his flat in Shanti Sadan on Peddar Road and in spite of Lataji, Ashaji and Rafi saab being such famous singers, they would go to his place to rehearse.

Then there was RD Burman. Pancham was a mad cook! Ashaji and he would have cooking contests. She's an excellent cook too. Whenever we were recording, we would wait at the studio at the end of our session because we knew she would bring home-cooked food for us.

On the other hand, Pancham liked to make European dishes and cooked pork very well. He used to add tons of chillies. He had a passion for them and even grew green chillies. He would order the seeds from Burma, Singapore—various places—and plant them. The terrace of his garage was covered with pots of chilli plants. He crossbred them too. Your mouth would be on fire if you happened to eat any of his chillies.

Another person who was passionate about cooking was Salil Chowdhury. He would make the most delicious chicken curry and invite friends over to his house for a meal. His wife Sabita and brother-in-law, Jagdish, were not allowed to enter the kitchen while Salilda was cooking.

Roop Kumar Rathod is another marvellous cook. And Reewa, his daughter, is better than both her parents. One day she marinated a fish and sent it to me. She's so young but she loves cooking. I find many young people are not that keen on cooking any more.

I have always wanted to understand why great musicians have this passion for cooking.

NMK: I suppose cooking is therapeutic and relaxing. And you're creating something and giving pleasure. There's an element of improvisation too.

Do you enjoy cooking?

G: I can't even boil an egg! I can make tea for myself. And that's because I use a tea bag. [*both laugh*]

NMK: You have spent endless hours in recording studios— you must have met many session musicians.

G: I knew many of them. Great classical musicians like Hariprasad Chaurasia and Shivkumar Sharmaji used to play music for films. There was also Ronu Majumdar, another famous flute player. Ustad Sharafat Khan, the father of composers Sajid-Wajid, who played tabla for film music.

Maruti Rao Keer played the tabla for SD and later became RD Burman's close associate, starting with his first film *Chhote Nawab*. Maruti played the tabla on our song 'Shaam se aankh mein nami si hai.' There was Manohari Singh, who played alto saxophone and a wide variety of flutes. Pancham's close collaborators were Basudev

Chakravarty, Maruti Rao Keer, Manohari Singh, Bhanu Gupta and Sapan Chakraborty, who also sang in films. Their contribution to Pancham's work was tremendous.

I knew all those musicians. We were one team.

NMK: Did playback singers ever ask for your help with pronunciation when recording a song?

G: They would consult me. But recording technology has changed entirely. The string section is recorded separately, and so is the rhythm section, etc., etc. The musicians do not necessarily even know each other any more—a musician comes, plays and goes.

A less established singer will record the scratch version before the main playback singer records the song. It has all changed. These days I am not often called for a recording. That's why there are frequent mistakes in the pronunciation of 'kh', 'gh' etc. Most people have not studied Urdu today, so that is why there is this problem. It's not their fault.

NMK: You have written poems and song about Time, including the very popular 'Aane waala pal jaane waala hai'. I could translate this line as:

> The coming moment is about to pass
> This coming moment is bound to go
> The coming moment comes to go

G: It depends on what you want to stress. It could be 'Dekho, yeh pal jo aa raha hai, yeh chala jaayega' [The moment that is about to come will pass]. Your tone is different.

In 'this coming moment is bound to go,' there is a sense of warning. 'The coming moment is about to pass' has a sense of hurry, which is unintentional.

You could also be very matter-of-fact—the moment that comes must go. Keep what you said, 'the coming moment comes to go,' that works well.

NMK: Thank you. I think using 'coming' and 'then comes' gives the line an interesting rhythm.

> Aane waala pal jaane waala hai
> *The coming moment comes to go*
>
> Ho sake toh is mein zindagi bitaado
> *A lifetime could be filled in it*
>
> Pal jo ye jaane waala hai
> *This moment that's about to pass*

G: Use 'about to slip away.' As there is a sense of urgency. But the choice is yours. Both are good—pass or slip away.

> Pal jo ye jaane waala hai
> *This moment that's about to slip away*
>
> Ek baar yun mili masoom si kali
> *I once happened to meet an innocent bud*
>
> Khilte huey kaha khushbaash main chali
> *It blossomed and, leaving, it said,*
> *'Be happy'*

G: There is a giving of a blessing in this line. So you could also say, 'When it blossomed, she blessed me with a happy life.'

Dekha toh yahin hai, dhoonda toh nahin hai
If you see it, it's here.
Search for it, it's gone

Pal jo ye jaane waala hai
This moment that's about to slip away

G: Lovely. Very well translated. You can see I have written a 'wah!' on my copy. [*both laugh*]

Ek baar waqt se lamha gira kahin
Once a moment fell from Time somewhere

Vahaan daastaan mili, lamha kahin nahin
A story was found there but not the moment

Thoda sa hansa ke, thoda sa rula ke
It brought some laughter, brought some tears

Pal jo yeh jaane waala hai
This moment that's about to slip away

NMK: Over thirteen million people have watched this song clip on Youtube! 'Aane waala pal' is hugely popular and the perfect example of a song that touches everyone. No one wants certain moments in life to pass. But before you know it, they're gone.

Was it difficult to explain the song to Hrishikesh Mukherjee who directed *Golmaal*, I mean since Hindi/ Urdu was not his language?

G: I have managed to explain songs to AR Rahman, too! His language is Tamil. Hrishida's Hindi was good, so the only word I had to explain was 'khushbaash'. No one can know everything. For example, I have learned many English words from you.

NMK: Likewise. I've learned many Urdu words from you. I must add, if you don't know a particular expression in English, your instinct is spot on. If I suggest a word for the translation, you know at once…

G: … whether it is close to the original. And if it is not, is it close in spirit and intention?

NMK: Yes, that's right.

I read a recent interview of yours in which you said, 'A song belongs to a time and history.' Can you elaborate?

G: All creative works reflect their period and the personality of the artist. In the same way, film songs of a certain period should not be re-mixed because they represent their time. Take Naushad's compositions in *Mughal-e-Azam*, if we give his songs a faster beat, what have we done? We've ruined them.

Today you can create the set of Sheesh Mahal on a laptop whereas Asif saab had to have it built physically for 'Jab pyaar kiya toh darna kya.' The lighting of the set had to be precise otherwise the reflection of the camera and crew would have been seen in the glasswork.

NMK: I believe the art director, MK Syed, took over six weeks to build the set. The glass came from Belgium and special artisans were brought in from Jaipur. This song has many difficult shots—we see Anarkali's reflection in the glass ceiling as the song line plays, 'Chaaron taraf hai unka nazaara' [I am surrounded by the image of my beloved].

How brilliantly Asif saab and his team have executed the scene. The black and white film always had three reels in colour and that song was photographed in colour.

G: Yes. It was filmed at Mohan Studio where Bimalda also worked. You're right, 'Jab pyaar kiya...' was filmed in colour, but Asif saab did not conceive the whole film in colour. And if he had, he would have planned the lighting, set and costumes according to his own aesthetics. By having colourized the film recently, in this era, when he has long since passed away, you have erased the history of that period.

One must respect the past, respect the work and creators of that work. In the same way, if you changed the instruments Hemant Kumar used in his songs, you would take away the musical history of those times.

That is why I am against remixing and the colourization of black and white classics. The arts are a history of a civilization.

Do you agree with me?

NMK: Absolutely. The old songs and *Mughal-e-Azam* stand out as fine examples of a glorious time in Indian cinema. They should be left alone.

There is magic in black and white films, and I believe actors working in that period have gained immortality over actors working in colour. As the famous American film critic Roger Ebert said:

> 'Black and white movies present the deliberate absence of colour. This makes them less realistic than colour films, for the real world is in colour. They are more dreamlike, more pure, composed of shapes and forms and movements and light and shadow.'

The fact that *Mughal-e-Azam* was made in black and white adds to its enchanting, dreamlike world.

Did you ever meet K Asif?

G: Yes. I remember he used to hold his cigarette between his third and little finger and would take a long drag, then flick off the ash by clicking his fingers. He had pockmarks on his face and used to wear a shirt made of Bosky silk and a Latha cotton shalwar. He was a typical Punjabi. That was his style. I cannot forget his confident walk.

There was once a screening of the rush print of *Mughal-e-Azam*, so Asif saab called the producer, Shapoorji [Pallonji], to request the reels of the film be delivered to a cinema nearby. The producer responded by saying:

'Take the film in a taxi.'

Often travelling by taxi himself, when Asif saab heard the producer's answer, he took a long drag on his cigarette, flicked the ash away and declared:

> 'The print of *Mughal-e-Azam* does not travel in a taxi. Send it in the Chrysler!'

NMK: That's a man who can make *Mughal-e-Azam*!

Over the years you have won twenty Filmfare awards and thirty-one nominations for Best Lyrics in Hindi cinema. The latest nomination you received was for 'Aave re hichki' in Rakeysh Omprakash Mehra's *Mirzya* (2016). Shankar-Ehsaan-Loy composed the music.

How did you enjoy working with Rakeysh Mehra?

G: He is excellent at understanding when music and lyrics combine well. One of the best experiences for me has been writing for his films. You could call them musicals. No one else could have made a musical like *Mirzya.* From the start of the film to the end, the voice-over narrative is all in verse. I have just been working with him on his next film, *Mere Pyaare Prime Minister.* The way he approaches music reminds me of Guru Duttji.

Rakeysh has so much passion for filmmaking and is involved with every frame in his movies. He's a gentle person and a man of few words. He's a good listener and that's a rare quality. It's a pleasure working with Rakeysh Mehra.

NMK: What I find interesting is that he does not use lip-sync songs. In many of his films, including *Rang De Basanti* and *Mirzya,* the songs are played in the background.

G: Yes, that's right. The songs are used as narrative voices and are extensions of the story.

NMK: Can we talk about 'Aave re hichki' in *Mirzya*?

The song evokes the imagery of the desert—the leafless keekar tree, the dry pond—images that describe the state of the lonely lover. You once said the song was inspired by a Rajasthani folk song and the expression means something like 'someone is thinking of you.' The literal translation of 'Aave re hichki' is 'having the hiccups.' That will not work in English and sounds too silly. In some countries sneezing can suggest someone is thinking of you. But I have gone with the simple 'Thinking of you.' Is that all right?

G: Try 'Remembering you.' And keep the gender neutral so the song verses could be from the point of view of a girl or a boy.

Nidra mein kisne yaad kiyo re
Who stirred me in my sleep...

Jagaaye saari raina re
... kept me awake all night?

Pia jagaave, jiya jagaave, diya jagaave re
It was the lover, the heart, the earthen lamp

Aave re hichki
Remembering you

Sandesa aayo na, chitthiyaan bhijaayi
No message came, no letter came

Saawan mein sookhe naina re
My eyes are dry in the pouring rain

Talaiyya sookhi, keekar sookha, bheetar sookha re
The pond is dry, the keekar tree is dry,
dryness fills within

Aave re hichki ...
Remembering you

Dhoop mundhere chadh gayo dhola
The sun is high over the roof

Jal gayo saari chhaaon re
Burning all trace of shade

Aangan paar karoon main kaise
How shall I cross the courtyard?

Talve jale mere paaon ke
The soles of my feet will burn

Talaiyya sookhi, keekar sookha, bheetar sookha re ...

O meri jaaniya re
O life of mine

Shaam dhale jo chaand chadhe to
The evening falls, the moon rises

Phir na rulaaiyo re
Don't make me cry again

O meri jaaniya re
O life of mine

Meri jaan ki saugandh hai
Swear on my life

Harshvardhan Kapoor and Saiyami Kher in *Mirzya* (2016), directed by
Rakeysh Omprakash Mehra. *Photo courtesy ROM Pictures.*

Yaad na aaiyo re
Don't make me remember you

Pia jagaave, jiya jagaave, diya jagaave re
It was the lover, the heart, the earthen lamp

NMK: I was talking to director Shaad Ali once about the importance of songs in India's cultural life. He agreed with me and told me how thrilled he was that a song from one of his films had become part of the repertoire of wedding songs. He was talking about 'Kajra re' from his delightful 2005 film, *Bunty aur Babli.*

It is also a great example of the work of composers Shankar-Ehsaan-Loy and singers Alisha Chinai, Shankar Mahadevan and Javed Ali. The song starts with a doha.

Aisi nazar se dekha us zaalim ne chowk par
The way that cruel man eyed me
on the village square

Humne kaleja rakh diya chaaku ki nok par
My heart landed on a knife's edge

Mera chain-vain sab ujda, zaalim nazar hatta le
My peace of mind turned to dust.
Look away, O cruel one

Barbaad ho rahe hain ji, tere apne sheherwale
Your stare has ruined people
from your very own town

Meri angdai na ttoote tu aaja
May my yearning never cease.
Come to me

NMK: You wrote all the songs from Shaad Ali's first film, *Saathiya*. Is he a close friend?

G: I think of him as a young director—a young boy really. I used to meet him quite often in Chennai, because in those days he was working as Mani sir's assistant. Before I'd say goodbye, I would give him some pocket money just as a father would. That is the kind of affection I feel for him.

Shaad was brought up in a cultured, literary and artistic world in Lucknow. His father is Muzaffar Ali, someone seeped in Sufiana poetry. Shaad has a deep social conscience because his mother, Subhashini Ali, is a committed Communist and President of the All India Democratic Women's Association. His grandmother is the famous Captain Lakshmi Sahgal, a colleague of Subhash Chandra Bose. Lakshmiji stood in the presidential election in 2002 but lost to Abdul Kalam saab. She was a great social worker. That's the kind of pedigree Shaad has.

But I must say he fights with me as much as my daughter Meghna does. He insists I use certain words in the songs I write for him, and also suggests a few words that he has probably picked up from his father. [*laughs*]

Ultimately one sentence says it all—Shaad is very dear to me.

Kajra re
Your kohl-rimmed eyes

Kajra re, kajra re, tere kaare kaare naina
Your kohl-rimmed eyes, your dark black eyes

O mere naina, mere naina, mere naina judwa naina
My eyes, my eyes, these eyes of mine

Kajra re
Your kohl-rimmed eyes

Surme se likhe tere vaade, aankhon ki zabaani aate hain
Your promises written in kohl
speak the language of the eyes

Mere rumaalon pe lab tere baandh ke nishaani jaate hain
Your lips have left a mark on my handkerchief

(Shankar Mahadevan & Javed Ali)
Teri baaton mein kimaam ki khushboo hai
Your words have an intoxicating scent

Tera aana bhi garmiyon ki lu hai
You blow in like the hot summer wind

Aaja ttoote na, ttoote na angdai
May my yearning for you never cease.
Come to me

Kajra re…
Your kohl-rimmed eyes…

G: There are many duos in film music like Shankar-Jaikishan, Laxmikant-Pyarelal etc. Sometimes one would compose the songs and the other the background score. Pyarelalji used to do the background music but he'd compose songs too.

Here we have a unit of three—Shankar, Ehsaan and Loy—and they compose songs together. That's rare. You need a voice, music and rhythm. You can't separate these three elements. That is the most beautiful part of a composition. A songwriter is probably the fourth member!

These three musketeers are a wonderful unit. I think Shankar is a master at composing tunes to lyrics. He's so fast. He also writes some very interesting dummy lines that are sometimes quite amusing.

'Tu dil mera le ja main chappal pahen ke aayi' [Take my heart. I'm on my way, but first let me put on my sandals].

I think Shankar mesmerises audiences when he sings on the stage. What a threesome.

NMK: How did he approach the 'Kajra re' song?

G: When Shankar gave me the tune and the dummy words, he said:

'Change all the dummy words, Gulzar saab. But just don't change "Kajra re".'

'I have already written a similar song that Daler Mehndi has sung—"Kajra re nainawaale, naina teri Chambal de lootere" [Your kohl-lined eyes are no different from the dacoits of the Chambal valley].

'Gulzar saab, when I was having a shower this morning, I couldn't stop singing the words "Kajra re". I could not get them out of my head. Please keep them in the song.'

'You've had your shower and you're all fresh, so I'll use them.'

We both laughed. So the words 'Kajra re' came from Shankar Mahadevan.

NMK: Then you built the whole song on the eyes—what they do, what effect they have, etc.

I think it's very clever to use the word 'personal' in 'aankhein bhi kamaal karti hain, personal se sawaal karti hain.' The English slips in naturally and is so suggestive. I can't think of an equivalent in Hindustani that would work as well.

G: I believe this song became a hit because of Aishwarya Rai. She is totally responsible for its success. People would go to see the film all over the country, just to see her dance.

Aankhein bhi kamaal karti hain, personal se sawaal karti hain
Eyes work such wonders,
they ask such personal questions

Palkon ko utthaati bhi nahin, parde ka khayaal karti hain
Without raising her eyes,
mindful as she is of modesty

(Shankar Mahadevan & Javed Ali)
O mera gham toh kisi se bhi chhupta nahin
My sorrow cannot be hidden

Dard hota hai dard jab chubhta nahin
I still ache even though the pain has gone

Aaja ttoote na, ttoote na angdai
Come to me. May my yearning never cease

Kajra re ...

NMK: A completely different kind of song is 'Humko mann ki shakti dena.' Can you remind me how it was used in *Guddi*?

G: It's a prayer the schoolgirls in Hrishida's [Hrishikesh Mukherjee] film sing every morning at assembly. Jaya Bachchan—she was Jaya Bhaduri in those days—plays the young Guddi. She is late for school and rushes into the assembly. The teacher, who has seen Guddi enter, winks at her and gestures for her to lead the prayer. So, in the middle of the prayer, there's a bit of storytelling.

There's the line: 'Saath dein toh dharm ka, chalein toh dharm par,' and as you know 'dharm' means faith. Here, I am playing on a pun because Guddi is in love with the movie star Dharmendra. So this line has a double meaning—it talks about taking the right path and in the context of the movie it could also mean Dharmendra.

In spite of the song being a school prayer, you can always find space for humour. It has a touch of a cartoonist's type of humour, the kind you see in the Amul Butter hoardings around the city.

NMK: I once saw an Amul Butter hoarding showing four shirtless young men frolicking in the fields with the caption: 'Young de Basanti,' a witty reference to the film *Rang de Basanti,* which was all about youth culture.

G: I must credit the composer Vasant Desai for the lovely feel of the music. Did you know even today, 'Humko mann ki shakti dena' is still sung in many schools as a prayer?

NMK: The song reminded me of a hymn.

G: It is like a hymn. The other day we were in Shankar-Ehsaan-Loy's recording studio, working on Shaad Ali's film *OK Jaanu,* and Shankar Mahadevan asked:

> 'Gulzar saab, this song "Humko mann ki shakti dena," did you write it?'

Before I could say anything, Shaad added:

> 'No, no, it's a traditional song. It's a prayer we used to sing at school.'

Rakeysh Omprakash Mehra, who happened to be there, added: 'That's right. I heard it at school too. Maybe Gulzar saab decided to use it in *Guddi.*'

I listened to them very quietly and said:

> 'I wrote it for *Guddi.* It was written as a school prayer. It is not a traditional prayer.'

I once attended a function presided over by the eminent Hindi poet Kedarnath Singhji. He sadly passed away in March 2018. He was a very senior poet. At the function, he said,

'We all write to become popular and want to be taken seriously. But there are times when the author himself is left behind and his work goes beyond him. For example, when I heard students in a school singing Gulzar saab's song "Humko mann ki shakti dena," I asked them if they knew who had written the words. They said it was not a song, but a traditional prayer. The school children did not even know that it was Gulzar who had written the song they sang every day. Gulzar's work has a life beyond him.'

I was humbled by the compliment, especially as it came from Kedarnath Singhji. I had never thought of the song in that way.

You know 'Gore gore haathon mein mehendi racha ke' in Bimal Roy's *Parineeta*? Bharat Vyas wrote that song and the heroine's friends sing it in the film. Now it is sung at nearly every wedding in north India.

The same is true of 'Ek paisa de de, babu.' [A paisa for me, mister] In the old days when beggars asked for alms, they used to sing these lines. Most people do not know that Prem Dhawan wrote them. His words became the cry of the mendicant.

There are countless songs sung by Lataji and Rafi saab that have become a part of our culture and psyche.

NMK: Coming to the translation of 'Humko mann ki shakti dena.' There are many ways of translating 'Mann vijay karein …'

G: 'Doosron ki jai se pehle khud ko jai karein'—why not try 'before conquering others, we must conquer ourselves?'

NMK: I think 'conquering' sounds slightly battle-like? Can we soften it and say 'prevail upon' or 'win over?'

G: 'Win over' is okay. How does that sound? Read it to me.

> Humko mann ki shakti dena mann vijay karein
> *Give us the strength to win victory over the self*

G: Later there is the line 'Doston se bhool ho toh maaf kar sakein' [forgive friends for their mistakes].

'Jhoot se bache rahein, sach ka dum bharein.' Here, 'dum' is not 'the breath'—that is too literal. It means 'we must be on the side of the truth.' Something like 'escape lies and support the truth.' Now you can put it in your own words.

NMK: 'May we shun lies and uphold the Truth'?

> Humko mann ki shakti dena mann vijay karein
> *Give us strength to win victory over the self*
>
> Doosron ki jai se pehle, khud ko jai karein
> *Before we win over others,*
> *let us win victory over ourselves*
>
> Bhed-bhaav apne dil se saaf kar sakein
> *Let us cleanse our hearts of prejudice and bigotry*
>
> Humko mann ki shakti dena...
>
> Doston se bhool ho toh maaf kar sakein
> *Let us forgive friends if they make mistakes*

Jhoot se bache rahein sach ka dum bharein
Let us shun lies and uphold the Truth

Doosron ki jai se pehle khud ko jai karein
Before we win over others,
let us win victory over ourselves

Humko mann ki shakti dena...

Mushkilein padein toh hum pe itna karm kar
Look upon us with kindness if trouble befalls on us

Saath dein toh dharm ka, chalo chalein toh dharm par
Let us follow the path of faith and do our duty

Khud pe hausla rahe badi se na darein
Let us be courageous and fear not adversity

Doosron ki jai se pehle khud ko jai karein
Before we win over others,
let us win victory over ourselves

NMK: Film music has definitely established a new musical tradition in South Asia and, as you say, songs have a life beyond cinema.

G: The *Guddi* song is a good example of this phenomenon, but I don't mean to blow my own trumpet.

NMK: I think the poet Kedarnath Singhji has done that in your place. [*both laugh*]
    Who chose Vani Jairam to sing this song?

G: The composer Vasant Desai. He was a very independent-minded person.

He had a music room at Shivaji Park in Mumbai where we used to work. He was a pious, god-fearing man, deeply rooted in Maharashtran culture. He knew a lot about Maharashtran folk music and the nautanki tradition—I am talking about the lavani artists.

It was in his Shivaji Park music room that I first met Vani Jairam. During the breaks, I noticed she kept drawing a flower with a small stem and from that stem grew another flower. The moment she realized that I was watching her drawing the flowers, she quickly hid her notebook away. She reminded me of a schoolgirl.

NMK: Do you think Vani Jairam's singing has the temperament of a young girl like Guddi?

G: Yes, that's what Vasant Dada also believed. The rain song in *Guddi*, 'Bole re papihara' was in fact the first song she sang for the film. Vani was really very good.

NMK: Her voice suited the character that Jaya Bachchan played. I think she looks so sweet.

G: Who? Vani or Jaya?

NMK: Jayaji—Guddi!

G: Yes, she looked very sweet.

One day I narrated my short story 'Guddi' to Hrishida; he liked it and the story stayed with him as a possible film. A few months later he said:

'That story with a girl who is in love with a star…'
'You mean "Guddi?" I narrated it to you.'

'Oh yes, you were the one who narrated it.'

That was typical Hrishikesh Mukherjee.

'Come on, Hrishida, you know it was me.'

'Guddi' was the story of my sister, whom we called Jeet. Her real name is Surjeet Kaur. Jeet had this habit of cutting out pictures of Dilip Kumar from magazines and keeping them lovingly in her notebook. That gave me the idea of writing a short story about a young girl who is in love with a star.

I think 'Guddi' was published in the early 1960s and appeared in my first collection of short stories called *Chauras Raat* [The Square Night].

When Hrishida decided to make the short story into a film, I wrote the screenplay and dialogue.

NMK: How was *Guddi* cast?

G: I met Dimple in HS Rawail's house and she was like the character I had imagined. I knew Dimple wanted to be an actress, so I requested Hrishida to meet her, but he was undecided and the film kept getting stalled.

Every now and then he would tell Chhotu-da, his younger brother, DN Mukherjee, and me:

'There's a girl at the Pune Institute who is perfect for the role.'

Chhotu-da and I kept trying to find ways of encouraging Hrishida to start the film. One fine morning we insisted that he come with us in the car to visit a great location. That was the excuse we used. Hrishida picked up his walking stick and asked:

'How long will it take to get there?'

'Dada, come! What work do you have anyway? Let's go.'

I was at the wheel and we set off towards Pune. In those days you had to take the old road via Thane. The Mumbai-Pune Expressway did not exist then. On the way we decided to stop for some biryani at Taloja. By then Hrishida had guessed where we were going.

We finally got to Pune and went to the Film & Television Institute. We met Mr Murli, the FTII Director, and Hrishida explained to him that we had come to see Jaya Bhaduri. She was called to Mr Murli's office and in she came, wearing a ghaghra-choli. She looked like a sweet little girl. She had so much life about her. Jaya's energy came across immediately—and it was obvious to us that she had the honesty and innocence to play Guddi. The FTII director showed us her diploma film, then Hrishida talked to Jaya. We were very happy that he decided to cast her.

NMK: Her acting is excellent in the film. I believe her first role was in Satyajit Ray's *Mahanagar.*

G: That's right. She is a very talented actress. If I remember correctly, Amitabh was supposed to play the lead role in *Guddi.* But he left two days after the shoot started. Bojo [Samit Bhanja], a star from Calcutta replaced him. Bojo was a fine actor too. He had worked in the Bengali film *Apunjan,* on which I later based my film *Mere Apne.*

Another incident happened around *Guddi,* which I think is worth talking about. We were in Delhi in January 1971.

We wanted to see the the first day, first show screening to gauge the audience reaction, so we went to Delite cinema.

Near the end of *Guddi,* when Jaya sings a Surdas bhajan, the audience started hooting and laughing. We were mortified—that was the climax of the film! Hrishida came out of the cinema with Sippy saab [producer NC Sippy] and made a call to Mumbai to Ajitda [Ajit Banerjee], the art director, who was also Hrishida's brother-in-law. He instructed him to put up a set on the terrace of his own house and said he would return to Mumbai that same evening to re-shoot the ending. Hrishida could see the film had collapsed.

Sippy saab was game for anything. He was also Hrishida's business partner. So they went back to Mumbai and reshot the scene the next day. Instead of the Surdas bhajan, Jaya would now lip-sync to the song 'Aaja re pardesi' from Bimal Roy's *Madhumati*. It was a film that Hrishida had edited. I don't know how Hrishida suddenly thought of that song, but something clicked in his mind and he understood what needed to be done.

Once the song was ready, NC Sippy had the task of replacing the new scene into the negative and into all the prints already in circulation around India. Sippy saab was a marvellous, methodical producer and he set about it expertly. In a matter of days, he had managed everything.

That same film, which was drowning because of the last scene, became a huge hit. I have seen these kinds of miracles when working with Hrishida.

NMK: To replace the bhajan with an iconic song like 'Aaja re' was quick thinking on his part!

I am sure it was quite an innovative idea then. In those days, movies did not use songs from other films in the soundtrack, not as much as they do today. Quite often we hear an old song playing in the background of a new film. It evokes the past but more than that, an old classic song, when used effectively, can bring out associated emotions in the audience. I'm thinking of Professor Siras in *Aligarh*, listening to 'Aap ki nazaron ne samjha pyaar ke kaabil mujhe' [Your eyes tell me you think I am worthy of love]. The song takes on a whole new meaning, as Siras believes the words describe his own feelings.

G: I see what you're saying.

NMK: We have discussed the impact of your *Guddi* song and how it has become part of school life in India. When you were at school, what did you sing at assembly?

G: I was studying at M.B. Middle School in Sabzi Mandi, Delhi. At assembly we sang, 'Lab pe aati hai dua banke tamanna meri, zindagi sham'a ki soorat ho khudaaya meri,' which, roughly-translated, means 'My desires come to my lips in the form of prayer. O God, may my life be like a candle that lights the way for others.' Sir Allama Muhammad Iqbal, the poet laureate of Pakistan, wrote this.

We sang it at assembly every day before classes began. Allama Iqbal saab also wrote: 'Saare jahaan se achha Hindostan humaara' [Our India is better than the whole world].

I remember Emile Joshi in my tennis club saying: 'Gulzar saab, did you know this was written by a Muslim?'

With a smile, I said: 'He was not only a Muslim, but the poet laureate of Pakistan.'

'Why did he write this?'

'Go deeper into it, forget your prejudices, then you'll understand. The lines in the poem also say, "Mazhab nahin sikhaata aapas main bair rakhnaa, hindi hain hum vatan hai Hindostan humaara" [Religion does not teach us to bear grudges against one another. We are all Indians and India is our homeland].'

I tried to explain to Emile Joshi that when the poet wrote this in the early 1900s, he was not thinking in terms of India and Pakistan. Pakistan is a later phenomenon. The poet's thinking was beyond all that. His words are about human beings and their aim was to encourage us not to harbour prejudice. Those poets were masters.

NMK: Most certainly.

You have worked with many directors in popular cinema. I believe you worked with some New Cinema directors too?

G: Sometime in the early 90s, I wrote the script and the dialogue for Kumar Shahani's film *Kasba*. We used to sit in Cozy Home, an apartment block on Pali Hill where I had an office. I wrote a song for Kumar's earlier film *Tarang*, which was composed by a fine and most unusual composer, Vanraj Bhatia. He would play ragas on the piano. It was an experience listening to him.

I remember once, a group of us, including Shyam Benegal and Smita Patil, were attending the Moscow Film Festival. Smita Patil was a lovely person. What an actress and such a good human being. One day the festival organizers decided to take us on a tour of Samarkand. During the tour I told Shyam Benegal that I wanted to assist him on a film and assured him I was completely serious and had been trained by a very great filmmaker, Bimal Roy. I found the stories of the New Cinema films close to literature, so I wanted to know more about that process. Shyam babu laughed and said:

'I have seen *Gharonda* and liked the screenplay that you wrote for it. I like your screenplays. We'll see.'

Smita Patil immediately asked: 'Gulzar saab, why do you need to assist him?'

We carried on chatting as we sat in front of the famous Bibi-Khanym mosque in Samarkand, watching a man sharpening knives at a short distance. Sparks would fly out from his grinding wheel as the knife hit it. You know the kind?

NMK: It's the old traditional way. Isn't it funny how some images stay with you forever?

Coming back to Shyam Benegal, did you ever get to work with him?

G: Some years later, he asked me to write the songs for *Mammo*. And I wrote 'Hazaar baar ruke hum, hazaar baar chale.' Vanraj Bhatia composed the ghazal and Jagjit Singh

A poster of *Gharaonda* (1970) starring Amol Palekar and Zarina Wahab, with screenplay and lyrics by Gulzar.

sang it. The song was talking indirectly about the divide between India and Pakistan.

That was the only chance Shyam Benegal gave me to work with him and I said: 'Shyam babu, you have finally given me a break.'

As usual, he laughed. He is a warm and affectionate person. Perhaps, 'Shyam se shikaayat toh yeh rahegi meri [That's perhaps that's the one complaint I have against Shyam Benegal].

NMK: Did you know Mani Kaul?

G: We once spent two days together at the Film Institute in Pune.

We discussed cinema. My feeling was that most films are a mixture of reality and illusion. I admitted I did not understand Mani's films, and asked myself why the sound seemed out of sync. I wasn't sure whether his films were before their time, or if I had to learn more about cinema.

Likewise when I saw Picasso's paintings, I wondered why the eyes or nose were not where they should be. Later I understood that a realistic portrait soon becomes boring because the object is always the same, whereas Picasso's paintings grew on me—you get involved with them and keep finding new interpretations.

When I dream, the images are not in sync. But they have a reality because they come from me. Dreams are born out of reality, from lived experiences. So, Mani's films are a dreamlike interpretation of reality. Mani looked up at me and said:

'Gulzar saab, I wish we had talked sooner, then I would've understood my films better.'

We both laughed. I really enjoyed his company.

Years later, I was given an award by Osian's. The citation was painted and handwritten by Mani Kaul. I treasured it but sadly, it got damaged. It was a loss for me. It was such a pleasure spending time with him. He spoke excellent Hindi and Urdu. He was related to the actor Raaj Kumar and was Mahesh Kaul's nephew.

Mani Kaul once spoke about Raaj Kumar's reaction to *Ashad ka ek Din.* He imitated the actor's voice and his famous style of speaking:

'Arey mian, koi dhang ki film banaiyye jisme koi zabaan ho. Yahaan koi bolta hai toh hont hilte nahin' [Make a proper film where there is some dialogue. Here, people are speaking but their lips aren't moving].

NMK: [*both laugh*] That's very funny.

The films you've directed have very different themes. I wanted to talk about *Meera,* which was released in 1979. When you decided to make the film, why did you choose Pandit Ravi Shankar as composer? That was an unusual choice, was it not?

G: You know the statement: 'I believe you, but I am not convinced.' And so I believed Lataji when she said:

'I don't want to sing in *Meera* because I have just made an album featuring Meera's bhajans composed by Hridaynath [Mangeshkar].'

I believed her, but I was not convinced. And because Lataji was not singing, Laxmikant-Pyarelal, the original composers for the film, decided they did not want to do the music. That was a big problem because we had already built the sets and I had to start shooting.

Pancham did not want to compose the music either because of his relations with Ashaji. He did not want to get involved. You know my closeness to Pancham, so his refusal implied something more than he was willing to say. I believed everyone but was not convinced. The result was no music director wanted to touch my film.

I've been fortunate to have worked with many good producers when I was directing films. People who have trusted me. The same was true of Premji, my producer for *Meera*. I was struggling to find a composer for the film and asked him:

'Can we get Pandit Ravi Shankarji?'

'Of course! But he's in America.'

Premji suggested we contact him through the producer Hiten Choudhury who used to work with Bimalda and was a good friend of Pandit Ravi Shankar. Hitenda used to call Panditji by his first name 'Robi.' When he managed to speak to Panditji, he said he would do the film if he liked the script. So Premji asked me to go with Hiten Choudhury and meet Panditji in New York. That was my first trip to America. It was the first time that I met Panditji. Of course, I had seen him in concert a number of times before that.

When we arrived in New York, sometime in the summer

of 1976, we went straight to the hotel he had arranged for us. Panditji said he would meet us the next day on his return from a concert in another city. When I first caught sight of Pandit Ravi Shankar entering the hotel lobby, he was wearing his travel clothes—a coloured bush shirt and jeans. That was not the image I had of him. After that, I never saw him wearing jeans again. [*laughs*]

Panditji was a very lively, good-humoured and large-hearted person. I gave him the script of *Meera* and asked if he would like me to read it to him, as is the usual practice in India. But he said he would read it himself. He read it overnight and the next morning he told me he had liked the script very much, adding: 'I'll do it, but who is going to sing?'

'Lataji is not going to sing.'

I explained the situation to Panditji who asked me to talk to Lataji again and ask her whether we could go with Vani Jairam. I was fine with his choice of Vani.

Coincidentally, Lataji happened to be in America, and was staying at the Watergate Hotel in Washington. She was on tour with the great playback singer Mukeshji and his son Nitin. The next day I called the hotel and got through to their room.

'Nitin?'

'Main Nitin ka baap bol raha hoon, Gulzar' [Gulzar, this is not Nitin, this is his father speaking].

Their voices were so alike, that's why I got confused. I spoke to Mukeshji and asked him for Lataji's room number. When I got through to her, she said:

'No problem if Vani Jairam sings for your film.'

How could I ever have imagined that would be the last time I would speak to Mukeshji? He never returned to India. He passed away in Detroit during that 1976 tour. Strange coincidences keep happening in life.

NMK: Did you return home immediately after your 1976 meeting with Pandit Ravi Shankar?

G: No, I stayed for a while in the States and accompanied him to various cities where he was performing. I remember attending a dusk-to-dawn concert in a church. Before I left for India, he said:

> 'I'll come there in September and start work on your film.'

I was keen that we complete the recording as soon as possible, as I had to start filming. The sets were ready.

It was a great experience spending time with Panditji. During that same trip I met Deepti Naval. She was working for a radio station and came to interview me. She had long hair—that is the image of her that has stayed with me. As she got up to leave, she said:

'Don't tell anyone, but I want to work in films.'

Whenever I see her I tease her:

'Don't tell anyone, but I want to work in films.'

Maybe her parents did not approve, I don't know. I also met Sunil Dutt there whom I knew from Mumbai.

NMK: Was Ustad Allarakha in America then?

G: Yes—he was accompanying Panditji in all his concerts. Khansaab used to talk to me in Punjabi.

It was during that trip, as I mentioned, that I enjoyed mutton curry made by Khansaab's own hand. One day, in the apartment where they were staying, Allarakha saab was teaching an American student the tabla. He was reciting the bols to her and she was playing—all this was happening while he was stirring the pot. On the 'sum,' he slammed the lid of the pot down—'Dhaa!' It was lovely!

He was a wonderful person. I was lucky to have met that generation of artists and to have worked with such stalwarts. I am really very fortunate.

NMK: How did the recordings for *Meera* go?

G: In nine days Raviji had recorded about 14-16 pieces and nine bhajans at Mehboob Recording studio in Bandra. He was such a disciplined man. I believe discipline is the force behind every great man.

NMK: Did Pandit Ravi Shankar enjoy working with Vani Jairam?

G: He had complete faith in her. She could remember every note by heart and was meticulous. It's no small feat to achieve the status that she did. For some reason she was pushed away from the Hindi film industry but made her name in the south. That's where she lives now.

NMK: Which of the bhajans in *Meera* come to mind now?

G: 'Baala main bairaagan hoongi' is a fantastic song. 'Mere toh giridhar gopal doosro na koi' is very special. It's in Braj Bhasha.

NMK: V.K. Subramaniam in his 2011 book, *Mystic Songs of Meera*, says, 'Mere toh giridhar gopal doosro na koi' is based on the Raga Jinjoti. Did you discuss the ragas Ravi Shankar would use?

G: No, I know nothing about ragas. It was entirely his choice. First of all, it would have been foolish on my part to have interfered and questioned him. He was a true master. And if you study the music of *Meera*, it's like a textbook for classical music students. All the bhajans are based on ragas. The music exudes a feeling of purity.

NMK: There are many translations of this bhajan on the Net and some are very good. I have only translated the first verse here.

> Mere toh giridhar gopal doosro na koi
> *For me there is only giridhar gopal*
> *and none other*
>
> Jaake sar mod mukutt mero pati vohi
> *A peacock-feather crown on His head*
> *is my husband*
>
> Mere toh giridhar gopal doosro na koi
> *For me there is only giridhar gopal*
> *and none other*

Hema Malini in Gulzar's *Meera* (1979).

The translation is quite meaningless without the reader knowing the context of Meera's life and her unconditional love for Lord Krishna.

Why did you make this film?

G: I was attracted to the personality of Meera and the times in which she lived. She had her own sense of values and morals. She was a liberated woman, yet you can see, 400 years later, women are still struggling for their place in society. Even today when a girl gets married, quite often her religion has to be that of her husband. The woman must do the converting, not the man. But Meera remained a Vaishnav.

The primary reason for me to do the film was the idea of making a biography. To imagine the life of someone who had lived a mere 300–400 years ago—a person whose story has now become mythology. All sorts of spiritual and miraculous feats are attached to her name. Meera is considered a myth today but she was also a flesh-and-blood person. So I was curious. Why not show her human side? She was a poetess and her poetry was so attractive and direct, especially when she describes her love for Lord Krishna. To me, she was an example in many ways. She had spirit and devotion.

The other reason I made *Meera* was that it coincided with the Year of the Woman and she was clearly a wonderful subject. When my producer, Premji, offered the film to me to direct, Hema Malini had already been cast in the lead role. That was fine by me.

When it came to creating the image and character of Meera, I could see how well Hema fitted the role—she has a royal presence. And I could imagine her as a leader. Her stature resembles a Rajput woman of standing.

NMK: What were the challenges of working on the film's music?

G: When he started to think of the composition of 'Main toh prem deewaani mera dard na jaane koi,' Pandit Ravi Shankar said:

'It is very difficult to do better than Madan Mohanji's tune of this bhajan.'

That's another example of a song that has gone beyond the composer and has become iconic. It was the last song in my film and Ravi Shankarji composed it in his own style.

NMK: You also worked with another classical musician, Zakir Hussain.

G: Zakir saab! He's very handsome, always was and always will be. He has a very open nature. He says what he thinks and is transparent in his way of dealing with the world. I think he has inherited that transparency and spontaneity from his parents—they were honest and straightforward people with great humility. The other day, at your Zakir Hussain book launch, you could see the respect with which he greeted people. He is such a renowned, celebrated person, yet he has stayed humble.

In 2003, we worked together on a ballet called

Pinocchio, which was later revived by Salim Arif. As you know, *Pinocchio* is a very famous Italian story written in 1883 by Carlo Collodi. The story has been adapted into a great many languages but it was never translated into Hindi or Urdu, so I thought why not try? Then the dancer/choreographer Bhashwati Misra, who is related to Birju Maharajji's family, got in touch with me saying she wanted to produce it as a dance piece. She said she would perform it along with two hundred children who were training in kathak. So Bhashwati produced a fabulous show.

When we were discussing the music, Birju Maharajji, who knew Zakir saab, suggested his name to us. So we got in touch with Zakir saab who said he would have to read the script first. He was in America so we could not sit face to face. We had a few sittings over the phone. It's funny we still call these 'music sittings,' even though it's more like being suspended in space!

At one point, Zakir saab wanted me to read out some lines to him because he thought they did not have a metre and sounded like prose. When I read, 'Tu jo mera beta hota, main tujhe Pinocchio pukaarta,' he could instantly identify the metre.

I explained that I wanted every character to speak in a different metre so I had changed it accordingly. For example, the narrator had his own metre, etc. After all, in real life we all speak with a different cadence. Zakir saab liked the idea of switching metres. But he also added that he was busy:

'I am travelling so I'll work out the basic music and rhythms, give them to my brother Taufiq, and if you like the tunes, Taufiq and I will work on them. Is that all right, Gulzar saab?'

I said, 'First of all, I am no one to approve a tune. I can only react and tell you how it sounds. However, the choreographer may have some comments.'

Then Taufiq, Bhashwati and I worked together. She would make suggestions about the beats that worked well with her choreography—I don't have a clue about dance. She would hear the music and count in her own system. I attended the recording of the ballet at Taufiq's studio, so the pronunciation would be correct. There were many voices involved.

I also worked with Taufiq again. It was for a biopic called *Aami*, which was loosely based on the life of Kamala Das, the great poetess and writer from Kerala.

I met Kamala Das at a function in Delhi when 'Little Magazine,' run by Amartya Sen's daughter Antara Dev Sen, was giving her a Lifetime Achievement award. Girish Karnad was presiding over the ceremony and they asked me to come to Delhi to present her with the award.

She was very charming. She would say whatever crossed her mind. I found a great similarity between her and the Urdu writer Ismat Chughtai. In those days, women had no voice—they were supposed to be coy, modest and silent. Kamala Das's writing was bold and courageous. I admired her a lot. In later life, she converted to Islam and became known as Kamala Surraya. Just like Ismat Apa [Ismat Chughtai], I feel these two great women were beyond religion.

When we were working on *Aami*, Taufiq was happy to create the tune on the words:

'Gulzar saab, aap mujhe alfaaz de dijiye. Abbaji bhi aise hi karte thhe, hum bhi aadi hai shayari ke' [Please give the words to me. My father used to compose the tune on the words as well. I understand poetry].

There was a song beautifully sung by Roop Kumar Rathod in *Aami* describing her falling in love with a younger man. To understand the word meaning, you have to take into account the second line first:

Aadhi raat mein ek nabeena roz chiraag jalaata hai
In the middle of the night a blind man lights a lamp

Rooh ke sannatte se koi jab awaaz lagaata hai
I hear a call from the silence of my soul

Aawaz na aayi kadmon ki, koi aaya hai mehsoos hua
I hear no footsteps yet feel someone approaching

Koi paas se ho kar guzra hai, ek saaya sa mehsoos hua
I feel a presence pass me like a passing shadow

Koi rooh ko roshan kar jaata hai
It lights my soul as it brushes past me

NMK: So the blind man is 'love' that takes her by surprise?

G: Yes, and 'aadhi raat' here means 'mid-life.' The fourth line describes her encounter with love.

It was lovely to have had the opportunity of working with Ustad Allarakha and then his sons Zakir and Taufiq.

NMK: Another of the many composers you have collaborated with is Anu Malik—you worked on *Fiza, Aks, Asoka, Filhaal* and *Jaaneman.* You also appeared in *Wajood* presenting an award—a film with Anu Malik's music.

G: Anu Malik is a very prolific music director. He has written great music for *Asoka* and Bosky's *Filhaal,* a film with some of his finest compositions. 'Bosky' is the nickname of my daughter Meghna.

Take the word 'filhaal' [in the meantime]. I didn't think I could use it in a song very easily, but Meghna insisted. We were working together not as father-daughter, but as lyricist-director. So you must follow the director's orders:

'I want a song to sum up the film and that's how the word "filhaal" must be used.'

I explained the word was not very musical, and that's when Anu intervened:

'Gulzar saab, usko musical banana mera kaam hai, aap likh ke de dijiye' [It is my job to make it musical. You write the words and give them to me].

What a beautiful way of putting it! So I asked Meghna:

'What do you want to say in this song?'

'I am addressing life. "I have seen the happy and sad times you have given me, I have seen ups and downs, but this moment belongs to me, let me live this moment— Filhaal mujhko ye lamha jee lene de."'

I worked on the line 'Ye lamha filhaal jee lene de' and Anu immediately composed the tune. Hats off to him for that melody. He made the words sound musical. It's a good song. Ashaji sang it.

NMK: You also wrote the songs for Meghna's 2015 film *Talvar*.

G: There are three songs in the film. Meghna can be a difficult director to work with. She rejected four versions of a song that Vishal had composed and I had written for *Talvar*, before finally approving 'Jis din aakaash bedaag hoga.' She said the reason she rejected the previous versions was their mood of romance and those were not what she wanted. Children can be difficult to work with [*smiles*]. When we came up with 'Jis din aakaash bedaag hoga,' Vishal and I realized how right she was.

I enjoy working with her because she knows what she wants. As a lyricist, I admire this quality in her. Meghna is a very focused director. She is not a newcomer and understands filmmaking well.

> Jis din aakaash bedaag hoga
> *The day the open sky is spotless*
>
> Chehra chaand ka saaf hoga
> *The day the face of the moon is scarless*
>
> Jis din samay ne aankhein kholin,
> Insaaf insaaf insaaf hoga
> *The day Time opens its eyes,*
> *justice will be done*

Behta kya aankh mein ummeed nahin hai
*Why would the eye tear up
when all hope has gone?*

Aansoo ka mol toh hai, khareed nahin hai
Tears have much value but no buyers

Taraazu utthega toh insaaf hoga
Insaaf insaaf insaaf hoga
*The day the scales of justice tip,
justice will be done*

Behti nadiyaan rukti nahin hai
Flowing rivers never stop

Doobo doobo tairo tairo doobo
Drown, drown, swim, swim, drown

Toh bhi mukti nahin hai
Yet you will not be freed

Gardan par hai karz lahu ka
The debt of blood is repaid with blood

Gardan de kar hi maaf hoga
Insaaf insaaf insaaf hoga
*You'll be pardoned when your head rolls.
Justice will be done*

NMK: Can you help me with the new song you've written for Meghna's new film *Raazi*? How would you translate 'pur paich'?

G: There is a line by TS Eliot: 'Streets that follow like a tedious argument.' What an expression! I borrowed this from Eliot when I wrote on Ghalib. Of course, I have credited TS Eliot.

'Ballimaran ke mohalle ki voh pechida dalilon ki si galiyan...' [Those streets of Ballimaran resemble tedious arguments]

So 'pechida' is from 'pur paich'.

Pur paich hain raahein jeene ki
Winding are the roads of life

Kismat ik tedhi baazi hai
Fate is a crooked roll of dice

Tum haath pakad lo iraade ka
Let intentions lead the way

Raah seedhi hai agar dil raazi hai
*The road ahead is clear,
if your heart is so inclined*

Lagan ki baazi hai
Your dedication is at stake

Chott bhi taazi hai
The wound is fresh

Laga de daav par dil
Gamble your heart away

Agar dil raazi hai
If the heart is so inclined

Kahaan le jaaye dil
Where will the heart lead you?

Jo hadh hai behadh hai
The limit is limitless

Lagan mein jaan jaaye
Commitment may take your life

Vahin toh sarhad hai
There, at the edge

Adhoora aage hai
The future is wide open

Mukammil maazi hai
The past is shut tight

Laga de daav par dil agar dil raazi hai
Gamble your heart away,
if your heart is so inclined

Havaaein dekh kar chalna
Mind the gust of the wind

Na mitti par kadam rakhna
Do not step on the ground

Nishaan reh jaaenge neeche
Lest you leave behind telltale footsteps

Khud apni aag mein jalna
Your conscience is up in flames

Lagan ki baazi hai
Commitment may take your life

Chott bhi taazi hai
The wound is fresh

Laga de daav par dil agar dil raazi hai
Gamble your heart away,
if your heart is so inclined

NMK: I'm grateful to Meghna for providing some of the line translations.

Generally composers are subject of discussion after they retire or when they have passed on. I feel it would be good to talk about some of the current composers.

G: We have talked about AR Rahman. He is at the top of this list but there are others like Shantanu Moitra. He hardly works in film, though the music he composed for *Parineeta* and 3 *Idiots* has been much appreciated. He spends much of his time performing concerts and composing jingles for ads. I worked with him on the music for the Tagore songs that I've translated into Hindi. Shreya Ghoshal and Shaan sang them beautifully. So it ended up being a trio of Bengalis—Shantanu, Shaan and Shreya.

Bengalis are very particular about everything associated with Tagore. For example, his songs are supposed to have only the Rabindra Sangeet style of music, composed by Tagore himself. But times have changed and there are new approaches to composition. Keeping the ambience of Rabindra Sangeet, Shantanu Moitra has modernized the singing of Tagore. He experiments in orchestration and stands apart for his creation of different musical moods.

NMK: He reminds me of Salil Chowdhury.

G: You're right. He has that touch of Salilda in his use of the musical scales. Shantanu Moitra is a truly modern composer.

The other composer who is also very unusual—and with whom I have worked—is Sandesh Shandilya. I did *Dus Tola* with him. Ajoy Varma, the grandson of Raja Ravi Varma, directed *Dus Tola*. He made three beautiful films based on three short stories and he always uses Sandesh Shandilya's compositions.

Sandesh's tunes are melodious. He has a modest temperament and keeps a low profile. He composes music only when he feels like it and is skilled at creating tunes that suit the narrative. He composed some of the songs in Karan Johar's *Kabhi Khushi Kabhi Gham*, including 'Suraj hua maddham.'

Sandesh has recently been invited to Hollywood to work on a film there. Like Rahman, he's now working on international projects.

There's another interesting composer—Simaab Sen. I knew his father, Sanjeev Sen, a music arranger who used to play rhythms for Pancham. His grandfather, Jamal Sen, composed music for Kamal Amrohi's *Daera* and Kidar Sharma's *Shokhiyan*. I first met Simaab when he was working as an arranger for Vishal's early films.

When Vishal and I went back to Lahore to record Rahat bhai for another song, Simaab accompanied us. From Lahore we planned to go to Karachi. But Simaab was not keen to come with us so we suggested he go home via the Wagah border. He was anxious about crossing it alone. A close friend, the producer Hassan Zia, whose film *Wrong No.* was a big hit in Pakistan, said he would take Simaab to the border—but he himself would not cross into India because he was nervous of the people at immigration! However, Hassan Zia assured Simaab he would stand at the border till the young man crossed to the other side [*laughs*].

Hassan and Simaab became friends and, when he was producing his next film, he called Simaab to Dubai and asked him to compose the soundtrack. Simaab was uneasy about going to Pakistan so Hassan reassured him not to worry and said he would come to India or they could record in Dubai. Politics have created such a needless, silly climate of fear.

So that is how Simaab came to compose the music for the 2015 Pakistani film *Mehrunisa, V lub U*, directed by Yasir Nawaz. The word is spelt 'lub' because the main character cannot say 'love'.

Hassan Zia calls me 'babuji'. It's the same term he uses for his father. He wanted me to write the theme song but found discussing my fees awkward. In the end, Simaab explained everything to me and I agreed to write a song for *Mehrunisa, V lub U*.

It's the first song I've written for a Pakistani film. Hassan explained the song situation to me:

> '*Babuji, ek theme song hai—is basti ko clean karo isme bahut kachra hai, ganda bahut hai* [Clean up this neighbourhood, it is filthy]. The song must be a metaphor to clean up society. It is the hero's ambition to cleanse the world. Because of the environment in which they live, his wife, who is from the other part of Kashmir, cannot bear a child.'

I found it an interesting idea. Hassan added that they could not pay me, so I suggested he forget about the money and send me some *gur* [jaggery] from Pakistan, which he did. [*laughs*]

Simaab composed beautiful tunes for the three songs in the film and finally, I wrote lyrics for them all.

NMK: Can you share some verses of the *Mehrunisa* song?

G: Bedaar raho, taiyyaar raho.
Keep awake, be prepared

Chahe khwaab lage dushwaar lage
Bedaar raho taiyyaar raho
Whether or not this dream is a difficult dream.
Keep awake, be prepared

Gumsum na rehna jo kehna hai kehna
Don't stay silent, say what must be said

Ke din raat badlo zara
Change day to night

Haalat bhi badlegi, haalaat badlenge
aadaat badlo zara
Situations and circumstances will change.
Just change your habits

Ye zameen bhi tumhin se, aasman bhi tumhin se
kaayenaat ye badlo zara
The earth and sky belong to you.
Just change the universe

Tum ho toh zameen hai, tum hi se haseen hai
haalaat badlo zara
The earth's beauty comes from you.
Just change the circumstances

Shaakh sookhi ho toh ped se tod do
aag mein daal do, khaak kardo
Cut the branch off the tree if it is dry.
Let it burn to ashes

Koi makdi agar ganda karti ho ghar
dafn kar do zameen paak ho
If a spider's web soils your house,
bury it and purify your home

NMK: Have you faced any particular challenges when writing your most recent songs?

G: The songs in the 2017 film *Rangoon* were interesting because I tried to recreate a feeling of the 1940s in the lyrics. It was totally Vishal Bhardwaj's vision of a period film. The takiya kalaam [catchphrase] of the main character Julia [Kangana Ranaut] is 'Bloody hell'. She is always saying it in dialogue so Vishal suggested I use it in a song. The film included some British characters so the usage of English was not out of place.

The other *Rangoon* song 'Yeh ishq hai' is worth listening to. Rekha Bhardwaj has sung one version and Arjit Singh the other. It is a Sufiana type of song.

NMK: I read there are various meanings of the Arabic word 'suf'. One meaning is 'wool' and this is associated with the Prophet Mohammed's companions, who wore coarse woollen clothes as a form of penance—as some Christian monks do. Another meaning I found is 'safa' or 'pure'.

G: As I understand it, a Sufi is someone who leads the life of an ascetic—a simple and pure life of prayer and meditation. He does not go through a prophet or messenger, but speaks directly to the Almighty. A Sufi has a one-to-one conversation with Allah—an uninhibited, free address. You have 'ishq-e majazi' and 'ishq-e haqiqi,' which, roughly translated, mean 'worldly love' and 'love for the Divine.'

NMK: You write many Sufi songs, but you also write political songs like 'Hatt loottnewale'.

G: No one had tackled the theme of landgrabbing in a film song before, so I tried to write that kind of song for Vishal's 2013 film *Matru ki Bijli ka Mandola*.

Paani paani kuaan sambhal
O water, protect your well!

Jiski kheti uski zameen hai
The land belongs to the farmer
who sows the crop

Babaji ki dhauns nahin hai
No one can claim it by mere threats

Jiska ganna uski ganderi
Sugarcane billets belong
to the sugarcane owner

Hatt loottnewale
Clear off! You plunderers

Jiski maati uska maal, kuaan sambhal
What the land yields is mine.
Protect your well

Hum beej na denge
We will not give you seeds

Hum byaaj na denge
We will not pay interest

Kal ka karza aaj na denge
We will not clear old debts

Teri loha laathi nahin chalegi
Your rod and stick have lost their power

Teri hekadi haan ji nahin chalegi
Your arrogance will no longer hold sway

Hathoda hathoda hathoda aur daraati
The hammer and sickle now rule

Hatt loottnewale
Get lost! You plunderers

Raja teri sab sunte thhe
O King, we all once heeded your will

Raah se kankar chunte thhe
Removing the pebbles on your path

Jaag jaag ke raata-kata
Keeping awake all night

Par tere kambal bunte thhe
Weaving a blanket for you

Raja loottnewale
O King! You plunderer

Sun raja loottnewale mhaare raja
Hear us, O King! The ruler who robs us

O teri taanaashahi nahin chalne denge
We will put a stop to your tyranny

Apna morcha nahin ttalne denge
Our strike cannot be called off

Teri chhatri le kar nahin chalenge
*We will no longer walk by your side
carrying your umbrella*

Ab dhoop mein tere paaon jalenge
Now the sun can burn the soles
of your feet

Jo khode kuaan
The man who digs the well…

Jo khode kuaan uska hi paani
… is the rightful owner of its waters

Hatt loottnewale
Clear off! You plunderers

NMK: It's a powerful song. The hammer and sickle line says it all.

It is well known that many poets and lyricists of the past, such as Sahir and Shailendra, were members of the Communist Party and their Marxist thinking underlines some of their lyrics. Do you share their poilticial beliefs?

G: I am aware of politics, but I am not a political man. I follow an ideology in how I lead my life. I have definite convictions. You must be aware of things around you, and try not to compromise on your core values—this guides your behaviour.

Since India is a democratic country, every few years we are asked to vote. That is the moment to introspect and examine your beliefs. As such I don't believe in one political party but I do believe in people. I believed in Dutt saab [Sunil Dutt] and his sense of values. I knew he was an honest man. I believed in Atal Bihari Vajpayeeji. I grew up with leaders like Pandit Jawaharlal Nehru.

Vijaya Mehtaji once asked me: 'You are not a political man, yet you comment on politics. How come?'

'If politics nudge me, I have to react like a common man would and express my thoughts through my writings.'

NMK: Can I describe you as a nationalist?

G: I don't know how to define that. Political slogans do not prove I am a nationalist or a patriot. I love my country. Call me by any name you want. When I admire or criticize politics, I am not criticizing the country, but the governance.

I made these points in my song 'Jai Hind, Jai Hind' in *Hu Tu Tu*. The words speak of 'My history, my faith. My India, victory to India.' But the song is also questioning: 'Kyun jaati nahin bekaari meri, kyun jaati nahin bimaari meri.' [Why can we not be rid of unemployment? Why can we not remove disease?]. The song speaks of the overcast sky; how I look forward to the rains falling on my crops for a great harvest. But when the rain clouds appear, someone robs them. When I sow the seeds of the sun—someone eclipses the sun.

These lines are from the point of view of an Indian farmer; the trials and suffering a farmer must endure. Songs like these were written for films but they express my own concerns.

NMK: Although you say you are basically a patriot—your thinking shows a leaning towards the Left.

G: I don't deny that. I used to listen to Shailendraji and Balraj Sahni saab and members of the PWA—the Progressive Writers' Association—with great attention. They were a Leftist group and I grew up listening to them.

The basic ideas and values associated with the trials of the common man have stayed with me. My own life experience has been one of struggle. I came up the hard way. I have seen very difficult days. So I identify with songs that speak of the common man's struggle.

Sajid-Wajid composed a song in the 2011 film *Office Office* called 'Bada aam aadmi hai aam aadmi,' which describe the common man. He has been worn down, 'ghista gaya' [beaten down, worn away]. He has been constantly suppressed.

Bada aam aam hai aam aadmi
The common man is a very ordinary man

Kare naam naam badnaam aadmi
The very name is a name maligned

NMK: The line in which 'inch by inch' appears—is there no word in Urdu for 'inch'?

G: No, the words for measurements have come from the English language.

The other line in the song 'Ttopi kursi par Tom kahin'—'Crown here, Tom elsewhere'—is a reference to the British Raj.

Don't translate 'neta' [leader]. It works well to say 'Neta…nation.'

Aaloo jaise bhara hua hai
Bodies like empty jute sacks…

Jism ki khaali boriyon mein
… stuffed with potatoes

Yeh system pi jaata hai inhe
The system slurps them up

Cup mein kabhi kattoriyon mein
Sometimes from a cup,
sometimes from a saucer

Har shakhs ko yeh sarkaari danda
Like a skimmer, authority sifts
the common man…

Office office phaintta hai
… sending him from office to office

Iss common man ko har officer
The common man…

Football bana kar khelta hai
… is kicked about like a football
by the bureaucrat

Inch inch ghista rehta hai
Worn away inch by inch

Sadak pe chalta aam aadmi
Walking down the street is the common man

Chalaan yahaan aur form kahin
Receipt here, form there

Ttopi kursi par Tom kahin
Crown here, Tom elsewhere

Is desh ka kya kehna yaaro
What can be said about this country, friends?

Hai neta kahin aur qaum kahin
Neta here, Nation elsewhere

Sukhwinder has sung another song in *Office Office*, which also speaks of the common man. It's called 'Chala Mussaddi'. Mussaddi is a symbolic name in Urdu for the common man.

NMK: Could we talk about a different kind of song? The *Lekin* song 'Yaara seeli seeli,' composed by Hridaynath Mangeshkar. It's so unusual in tune and language.

G: I have done two films with Hridaynath and enjoyed the experience. He has worked a lot in Marathi cinema and composed some very fine music. He knows classical music extremely well and is greatly skilled in composing tunes on lyrics.

His body clock works the other way round than most people. He has dinner at three or four in the morning. His disciples come to learn music from him during the night, and then he goes to sleep and wakes up in the afternoon at about two. Raj Kapoor used to do that too!

Yaara seeli seeli birha ki raat ka jalna
O my love, the night of separation burns

NMK: I'm not sure what the word 'seeli' means.

G: It means damp.

NMK: Can we go with 'moist'?

G: Yes, it suggests the night of separation is moist with burning tears.

NMK: Will 'stinging tears' do? What about 'dhola'?

G: 'Dhola' is 'lover' in Rajasthani. The film is set in Rajasthan, hence this usage.

NMK: Will 'O my love' for 'yaara' work?

G: How about 'O dear'?

NMK: Can we avoid? 'O dear' can be interpreted as an exclamation of surprise or anguish—'Oh dear, I dropped the plate.'

Yaara seeli seeli birha ki raat ka jalna
O my love, the moist night of separation stings

O yaara seeli seeli, dhola seeli seeli
O tearful lover

Yeh bhi koi jeena hai
What kind of living is this?

Yeh bhi koi marna
What kind of dying is this?

Yaara seeli seeli birha ki raat ka jalna…

Ttooti hui choodiyon se jodun yeh kalaayi main
With broken bangles, I put my wrist back together

G: You got it right. Instead of repairing the broken bangles, it is the broken wrist she mends.

Pichhli gali mein jaane kya chhod aayi main
I do not know what I left behind in the past

Beeti hui galiyon se phir se guzarna
I must return to those days again

Yaara seeli seeli, dhola seeli seeli…

Pairon mein na saaya koi, sar pe na sai re
No shade on my feet, no God's protection

G: Instead of protection use 'shelter.' So you have shade and shelter.

Pairon mein na saaya, koi sar pe na sai re
No shade on my feet, no God's shelter

Mere saath jaaye na meri parchhayi re
Even my shadow has abandoned me

Baahar ujaala hai
Outside there's light

Andar veerana
Inside darkness

Yaara seeli seeli, dhola seeli seeli…

NMK: You have also worked with Ilaiyaraaja, the great composer from the South.

G: He wrote the music for one of Ajay Verma's films called *SRK* but it was never released.

Ilaiyaraaja is a master. I met him last year in Mumbai at a function held to honour him and celebrate his work in a thousand films.

NMK: You mentioned the title *SRK*—did the film have anything to do with Shah Rukh Khan?

G: No, the producer thought it was a very clever title! People have fascinations of their own.

NMK: How was working with Ilaiyaraaja?

G: He composes at great speed. He's the only music director I know who records the background music of each reel in one go. He has the full orchestra present and the musicians play their portions in consecutive order. Even if it means rehearsing for an hour, his background score is not recorded in fragmented pieces, which is the usual practice.

NMK: Do you mean that the music follows the timeline of the reel and the orchestra plays from start to finish—so the musical sections are played in one flow?

G: That's right. He's the only composer I've seen who works like this.

In 'Ae zindagi gale laga le' from the 1983 hit film *Sadma*, there was a small musical note I wanted to add to the end of the line 'Hai, na?'. Most people call him 'Raja' and so did I:

'Raja, at the end of the verse, can I turn this note into 'Hai, na?'

'Why not?'

Ae zindagi gale laga le
O life, hold me close

Hum ne bhi tere har ek gham ko
gale lagaaya hai, hai na?
I have embraced your every sorrow.
Isn't that so?

G: There was a moment when I got stuck—the words were just not working on the metre of the tune. Raja asked me for my lyrics and immediately recomposed the tune.

Rahman was his assistant in those days, and that's where we first met. Actually I did not recall that meeting, but Rahman reminded me. Then it came back to me. In those days, Rahman had long, curly hair.

NMK: Many composers past and present are non-Hindi speakers. How do they follow the phonetic pattern in a Hindi/Urdu song without understanding the language?

G: When we discuss the song we speak in English. English has become the link language between the many languages in India. So all difficult words can be explained.

I have noticed something when it comes to musicians. I wonder how they do it—take Lataji, she can sing a song in Dogri, Punjabi or Bengali without knowing any of those languages very well. She picks up the notes and tones with total ease. And this is true of many non-Hindi-speaking singers.

Rahman once asked me to give a Punjabi touch to the song 'Banjar hai sab banjar hai' from *Saathiya*, so I added the line, 'Mainda yaar mila de saiyyaan.' He sang the Punjabi without any difficulty.

> Banjar hai sab banjar hai
> *Surrounded by a wasteland*
>
> Hum dhoondne jab firdaus chale
> *I set out to find Paradise*
>
> Teri khoj taalaash mein, dekh piya
> *In search of you, my beloved*
>
> Hum kitne kale kos chale
> *See how many miles I have crossed*

NMK: When you write a song, do you ever think a particular line would work well in mid-shot or long shot?

G: That is not the role of a lyricist. The picturization is entirely the director's job or the choreographer's. But yes, images and visuals do come when we're writing and composing songs.

I wrote the dialogue and songs for Jabbar Patel's 1986 film *Musafir* and while Pancham, Jabbar Patel and I were working on 'Bahut raat hui, thak gaya hoon mujhe sone do' [It is late, let me sleep], Pancham asked if there was a river in the scene. I asked him to explain why and he said he wanted to add the call of a boatman between the verses.

This would look silly if the song was going to be picturized on a mountaintop—the visuals have to match the words.

If certain images come to you while working on a song, you tell the composer. So he can use an appropriate instrument. Creating songs is teamwork. It is not the result of one man's input. That is the beauty of cinema—working the scenes out together.

Don't forget the film song has to also make some impact outside the film itself. This makes the song popular. It has to be specific to the character yet universal, so it can stir the emotions of many.

NMK: Today's technology and methods of communication have helped connect music and musicians all around the world. And perhaps widened the choice of musical instruments?

G: The horizons have expanded. Indian composers are on a par with world musicians and they do use all kinds of instruments today. These choices were not available to earlier masters.

Everything has changed. Today when our heroines appear in a film, they say 'Hi!' There's no more of that coy, eyes-lowered 'Namaste-ji' [*both laugh*]. That time has long gone!

NMK: You have worked with several generations of composers. Who is the youngest?

G: Reewa, Roop Kumar Rathod's daughter. She has written some very fine classical tunes. She has a very modern take on music. The song we're working on is called 'Maula.' The way she addresses the Maula is not the way my generation would have done. That's the beauty of new ideas.

Maula, tu aisa kar de
O God, could You do this for me?

Thoda sa baadal bhar de
Fill the clouds with rain

Aftaab jo dekha kare
So when I see the sun…

G: Wait. Here we have the question of the point of view! It is the sun that has caught sight of her? Or the reverse?

NMK: I was confused. I thought it was 'I see the sun,' and not 'the sun sees me.' I see, it's the sun who sees me.

Aftaab jo dekha kare
The sun who sees me

Mujhko satrangi kar de
Makes me into a rainbow

Khushboo ke rang hain toh bata
Does fragrance have a colour?

Mehndi pehnoo ya mahuwa
Is it the colour of henna or a flower?

Uss ko jo bhaa jaayein toh bata
Tell me what would please him

Ishq ka koi rang bata
Tell me the colour of love

Dil ko mera dulha kar de
Make my heart a bridegroom

Maula, tu aisa kar de
O God, could You do this for me?

NMK: You have also worked with Reewa's father, Roop
Kumar Rathod.

G: Roop is also a great exponent of classical music and
a singer and composer. The tabla is his instrument. He
has made a wonderful album with Amjad Ali Khan saab
called *Vaada*. Roop took the bandishes composed by this
excellent sarodist and elaborated them musically.

The song 'Roz-e awwal' from the *Vaada* album has made
a mark. The song starts with me reciting some verses. It is a
kind of duet between Roop and me.

(Gulzar reciting)
Raat mein jab bhi meri aankh khule
Whenever I happen to wake up at night

Kuchh zara door ttehelne ke liye
Nange paaon hi nikal jaata hoon
I set out barefoot walking some distance

Akaash utar ke
Kehekashaan chhu ke nikalti hai jo ik pagdandi
I walk on a small path brushing past the Milky Way
descending from the sky

Apne pichhvaade ke santoori sitaare ki taraf
I walk towards bright Centaurus

Doodhiyaa taaron pe paaon rakhta, chalta rehta hoon
Stepping on the milky stars, I keep walking

Yahi soch ke main koi sayyaara agar jaagta mil jaaye kahin
Thinking if I bump into a planet awake somewhere

Ek padosi ki tarah paas bulaale shaayad aur kahe
Like a good neighbour, he may call out to me and say:

Aaj ki raat yahin reh jaao
Tum zameen par ho akele
Main yahaan tanha hoon
Stay with me tonight
You are alone on earth
And I am lonely too

NMK: This song was difficult to translate. Thank you for correcting my mistakes.

G: But it's turned out well.

I walk down the galaxy because I'm looking for another existence somewhere and hope I may come upon a planet that talks to me like a neighbour.

NMK: You have written a book on *Pluto*. Why do you have this fascination for astronomy?

G: If man who has lived all his life in a remote village and one day he lands up in a bustling city like Mumbai, imagine his reaction! He will naturally be intrigued by everything he sees.

Likewise, if you study the universe it's absolutely fascinating. There are families of planets and each one behaves in its own way. The galaxy is rotating in this vast space. There is so much noise and so much light. It's not dark up there. Fragmented meteors are travelling with gases around them. Sometimes a burning meteor descends to earth—we call it a shooting star—but it's a meteor. The sun that we know is a dwarf sun—can you imagine what a big sun is like? We may not believe it but we are not the centre of the universe. The earth is in the suburbs of a galaxy [*both laugh*].

You'll find books all over my house about the cosmos. My favourite website is the official NASA website. I am constantly looking for new images of space.

So the song 'Roz-e awwal' is about space travel.

(Roop Kumar Rathod)
Roz-e awwal hi se aawaara hoon, aawaara rahoonga
From time immemorial, forever the wanderer

Chaand taaron se guzarta hua banjaara rahoonga
Passing the moon and stars, forever the gypsy

(Gulzar reciting)
Chaand pe rukna aage khala hai
Mars se pehle tthandi fiza hai
Stop on the moon, there's a vacuum beyond.
A chill wind blows before you get to Mars

(Roop Kumar Rathod)
Ik jalta hua chalta hua sayyaara rahoonga
Like a burning planet, forever the traveller

Chaand taaron se guzarta hua banjaara rahoonga
Passing the moon and stars, forever the gypsy

Roz-e awwal hi se aawaara hoon, aawaara rahoonga
From time immemorial, forever a wanderer

(Gulzar reciting)
Ulkaaon se bach ke nikalna
Watch out! A meteor may crash into you

Comet ho toh pankh pakadna
Catch a comet's wing when it flies past

(Roop Kumar Rathod)
Noori raftaar se kaayenaat se main guzra karoonga
Travelling through the universe at the speed of light

Chaand taaron se guzarta hua banjaara rahoonga
Passing the moon and stars, forever the gypsy

Roz-e awwal hi se aawaara hoon, aawaara rahoonga
From time immemorial, forever the wanderer

NMK: I hope you approve of this translation. I have taken a different approach. Is it all right?

G: It's lovely. The steering wheel of a rocket, I have visited the cosmos with you. [*both laugh*]

NMK: We must speak about your fine ghazals that Jagjit Singh has sung.

G: There's Jagjit and Bhupinder [Bhupinder Singh]. Bhupi's first song with me was 'Beeti na bitai raina' from *Parichay*. He sang the songs in *Haqeeqat* and appeared in the film as well.

Jagjit and Bhupi were close friends of mine. I met them through my younger brother Trilochan and interacted with them as I did with Trilochan. Jagjit and Bhupi were like brothers to me.

It was Bhupi who arranged Jagjit's marriage to Chitra. He spent forty-five rupees on their wedding. They couldn't afford much because they were both struggling in those days and forty-five rupees was a lot of money. Within that same amount you could pay the priest, buy flowers and mithai!

Sometimes when Jagjit and Chitra fought bitterly, Bhupi would sort out the problem between them, reminding them that his forty-five rupees had better not go waste. Then their quarrel would turn into good humour. [*laughs*]

Bhupi knows how to sing a ghazal beautifully—he has a Sufiana spirit and his choice of poetry is of a higher level. He knows how much his voice moves me.

Tum apni aawaaz ka taaveez bana ke de do,
main pehen leta hoon
Make an amulet of your voice and I shall wear it.

NMK: What about Jagjit Singh's style of singing the ghazal?

G: That is legendary. Like Mehdi Hassan, he knew the 'mizaaj' [temperament] of the ghazal. I always say ghazal singing has a temperament and you have to know it. Unless you know that form of poetry, you really cannot sing a ghazal. In 'Sajda', the album we did together in 1991, for example, there are couplets sung by Lataji and Jagjit. His version sounds like a ghazal. Lataji's singing is perfect but it does not sound like a ghazal. It sounds like classical singing.

Jagjit had a wonderful rapport with audiences. He cast a spell on people. I used to call him Ghazaljit Singh.

Sometimes we would argue. And Jagjit would say:

'Aisa koi sher bolo jo dil ko lage' [Write me something that touches the heart].

'Main bahut nishaane lagaata hoon tere dil pe lagta nahin hai—kya karun?' [I have aimed many couplets at your heart but they do not seem to touch you—so what can I do?]

He used to say he did not always understand my poetry. He gave me the example of the ghazal 'Teri aawaaz sunaayi di hai. Ek parwaaz dikhai di hai' [I heard your voice. I saw the flight of a bird]. He asked me to explain the connection between the two lines.

'When the sound of a charming voice passes your ear, do you not see the flight of a glittering bird pass by?'

'Now that you've explained it to me, I understand the connection. But how to convey it to the audience?'

'The audience reacts emotionally to the words and the tune. They'll understand.'

NMK: There's that wonderful ghazal 'Shaam se aankh mein nami si hai.' Can we translate it?

Shaam se aankh mein nami si hai
As the evening falls, I feel my eyes moisten

Aaj phir aap ki kami si hai
Once again I feel your absence today

G: You can drop 'today.' The idea is there in 'once again.'

Dafn kar do humein ke saans mile
Bury me so that I may breathe again

Nabz kuchh der se thhami si hai
I feel my pulse slowing down

G: 'My pulse has stopped' is better. This thought is connected to the line before it, 'Bury me so that I can breathe again.' Don't involve the self when you translate 'iss ki aadat …'

Nabz kuchh der se thhami si hai
I feel my pulse stop

NMK: What about 'it shares this human habit'? Is that okay?

G: That's good.

Waqt rehta nahin kahin ttik kar
Time never stands still in any place

Iss ki aadat aadmi si hai
It shares this habit with us humans

With Jagjit Singh.

Koi rishta nahin raha phir bhi
Though no ties bind us

Ek tasleem laazmi si hai
Exchanging greetings is a must

G: The idea here is—I know there is no relationship between us any more but if we pass each other on the street, we must not forget to exchange a greeting. Good manners dictate it. You need the word 'must.'

Koi rishta nahin raha phir bhi
Though we are no longer together

Ek tasleem laazmi si hai
Exchanging greetings is a must

Shaam se aankh mein nami si hai
As evening falls, I feel my eyes moisten

Aaj phir aap ki kami si hai
I feel your absence once again

G: There is an interesting story about 'Shaam se aankh mein nami si hai.' This ghazal was born four times with four different music directors, each one of high repute, composing a tune on this mukhda.

The first was Salil Chowdhury, who was composing music for a film his younger brother, Babu Chowdhury, was to direct in the 1960s. I think the title was *Matti ki Devta*. Salilda asked me for a ghazal and I gave him this couplet, 'Shaam se aankh.' When he started composing the tune, he asked:

'Can I repeat these words, "nami nami si hai, kami kami si hai"? They would work better with the tune.'

I agreed and the song was recorded—it had this mukhda with different antaras. But the film was shelved and that was that.

Then my assistant, Meraj, whose first film, *Palkon ki Chhaon Mein,* was released in 1997, was starting a new movie. He had read the lines 'Shaam se…' somewhere and asked if he could use this ghazal. Laxmikant-Pyarelal were composing the music.

This was in the late 1970s. It was Laxmikant's turn to ask if he could repeat the words 'nami' and 'kami.' I recounted the Salilda incident to him and Laxmiji said:

'Usme humaari ginnat aur taal mein kuchh farak padta hai, is taal mein ye achcha aata hai' [By repeating the words, the number of beats changes. The song will sound good in this rhythm].

Sadly Meraj's film got shelved too.

Then some time in the late 1980s, when Pancham and I were making the non-film album 'Dil Padosi Hai,' I read a couplet of the same ghazal to him. He heard the history of the song:

'My friend, this couplet is very good, give it to me.'

'Look, both times the films were shelved, it might go wrong for you too.'

'I will not repeat the words "nami" and "kami". We'll be rid of the the jinx.'

And that is how it featured in 'Dil Padosi Hai,' but, surprisingly, this ghazal never found its way into a film.

Finally, in 1999, Jagjit read the ghazal in a book of mine and asked me if he could have the song. The story of the three music directors did not stop him.

'Female singers have sung this song in the previous versions, this time it will be a male voice. Please write new antaras for me.'

'Shaam se aankh mein nami si hai, aaj phir aap ki kami si hai' became one of Jagjit's most popular ghazals.

On one occasion, he suggested that while he was singing the song at a concert, I should join him on stage and recite my poems. We had not fixed a cue for me to enter, so I sat in the wings, waiting for a sign. Then I heard him singing 'Aap ki kami si hai' [I feel your absence] again and again. I could see a smile on the faces of the musicians, but I still did not understand what was going on and why Jagjit was repeating this line. Suddenly I realized that was my cue to go onto the stage. [*both laugh*]

Jagjit had this mischievous side. I never saw him get angry. I have seen Bhupi lose his cool but never Jagjit.

My association with Bhupi and Jagjit was very close. It's nice to talk about them in the same breath. We felt like one family—Jagjit and Chitra, Bhupi and Mitali. Now that Jagjit has left the family, we all miss him.

When I see Bhupi, we talk about Jagjit and we also talk about Pancham, because he was another family member.

NMK: I believe you recently recorded a new album with Bhupinder Singh.

With Bhupinder Singh.

G: Yes, it's called 'Dil Peer Hai'. I think it's a good title. Can I read you some lines, then you can translate? Rashid Khan and Shivangi Desai have sung this ghazal.

Kaun aayega ghani raat yeh sunsaan bahut hai
Who will come to me in this dark and lonely night?

Ek ummeed bhattakti hai pareshaan bahut hai
Only a wandering and troubled hope

Dil mein jab dard basey thhe toh guzar jaati
thheen shaamein
When pain dwelled in the heart, nights passed

Aaj sukoon aane laga hai toh viraan bahut hai
Now peace is here, emptiness overwhelms

Neend aati nahin aur need mein rehta hai hamesha
Sleep is elusive, drowsiness persists

Ishq khud apne hi andaaz pe hairaan bahut hai
Love is bewildered by its own ways

Tairte rehete hain jo aankhon ke paani mein hamesha
Still floating in my moist eyes…

Aise namkeen se kuchh logon se pehechaan bahut hai
… are some familiar beauties

Ishq ki loriyon mein dard ne thapkiyaan di thheen
The lullabies of Sorrow and Love once patted me to sleep

In buzurgon ka bada hone mein ehsaan bahut hai
Much is owed to these elders who raised me

NMK: I assume the two elders referred to in the last line are 'Sorrow' and 'Love.'

G: You're right.

In 'Dil Peer Hai' there is a very interesting folk-style song about a girl who is being married off and who has to leave her parents' home.

This is one of my favourite songs. Bhupi has composed it so well.

> Maiyya re bettiyon ke kaahe lagaaye bootte
> *Why did you plant daughters, mother?*
>
> Loriyaan jhootti teri lade bhi jhootte
> *Your lullabies and pampering were misleading*
>
> Kaahe paraayi kar di laadli, maiyya
> *Why turn your cherished child
> into a stranger, mother?*
>
> Baabula baabula re kaahe lagaaye bootte
> *Why did you plant daughters, father?*
>
> Kuaan bhi jhootta tera, daane bhi jhootte
> *Your water and your food were misleading*
>
> Kaahe paraayi kar di laadli, baabul
> *Why did you plant daughters, father?*
>
> Jo bhi kahe tu baabul voh hi karoongi main
> *Father, I will do as you say*
>
> Jo bhi kahegi maiyya, voh hi karoongi main
> *Mother, I will do as you say*

Aaj ke din doli rok le, baabul
Stop my palanquin for another day

Ghar ka peepal kuda karega, kaaga daal pe bole
The peepal tree will shed its dry leaves,
crows will caw from the branches

Roz bulaayegi gaiyya mohe sarson sang de chhole
As always the cow will demand chickpeas in her fodder

Roz bohaari karoongi, baabul
I'll sweep the house every day, father

Aaj ke din doli rok le, baabul
Stop my palanquin for another day

Saawan mein ye aangan maiyya soona lagega tohe
The house will feel lonely
in the coming monsoons, mother

Kiski mendhiyaan karegi maiyya, kaun sunaayega dohe
Whose hair will you braid?
Who will sing to you, mother?

Chulha chounka karoongi maiyya main
I will do all the cooking, mother

Aaj ke din doli rok le
Stop my palanquin for another day

NMK: It's such a moving song and describes so effectively
the feelings of a young woman being married off, probably
against her will.

Perhaps it is no coincidence that this song is a favourite of yours. A non-film album clearly allows you freedom because you do not need to restrict the vision of a song to match a filmic situation.

G: When you do any kind of writing routinely, you want something that liberates you. A composer feels the same way about compositions. It's relaxing to work without constraints, without limiting yourself to the language of a character. You can use words you would not normally use in a film song—because a film has to appeal to large audiences—so you try and use a vocabulary that reaches out to many.

NMK: Do you use a higher level of Urdu in your non-film songs?

G: No, I mean you still want to communicate but you don't mind if the album appeals to a smaller group of people. You are also free to lean more towards classical music. The non-film album is liberating.

NMK: Getting back to film music, the duet has always been a popular form. You've written many lovely duets but I particularly like the ones in *Guru*.

In 'O humdum,' you use the word 'beswaadi'. I don't think I've heard that word in a song before.

G: No, I haven't either [*smiles*]. But I liked the idea of a tasteless night.

You said you wanted to use 'without flavour'? Maybe it works better than tasteless. When you translate 'sautan' you can say 'rival'.

NMK: I might go with 'mistress' for 'sautan'.

(AR Rahman)
O humdum bin tere kya jeena
My love, what is life without you?

Tere bina beswaadi-beswaadi ratiyaan, o sajna
My love, without you nights are
without flavour...

Rukhi re o rukhi re
... so dull and dreary...

Kaattoon re katte katte na
... never seeming to pass.

Na ja chaakri ke maare
Don't go, on the pretext of work

Na ja sautan pukaare
Don't go, if your mistress calls

Saawan aayega toh poochhega, na ja re
When the rains come
they'll ask after you, don't go

Pheeki-pheeki beswaadi ye ratiyaan
Bland are these nights without flavour...

Kaattoon re, katte na katte na
... never seeming to pass

G: I imagined the face of the moon like an ashrafi—a gold coin. So without the beloved the moon's gold face appears fake. The next line is calling the moon a liar.

(Chinmayi)
Tere bina chaand ka sona khotta re
Without you, the gold face of the moon is fake

Peeli-peeli dhool udave, jhootta re
Spraying golden dust, the liar

(AR Rahman)
Tere bina sona peetal
Without you, gold is brass

NMK: I don't understand the next line.

G: 'Tere sang keekar peepal' means—'if you are with me the thorny keekar tree feels like a peepal.'

NMK: This not an exact translation, but could I replace 'keekar' with 'cactus'?

G: Yes. It's essentially the same idea.

Tere sang keekar peepal
*With you by my side
a cactus is a peepal tree*

Aaja kattein na ratiyaan
Come to me, the nights do not pass

NMK: The other fabulous *Guru* duet is 'Ae hairat-e aashiqui' sung by Hariharan and Alka Yagnik. Rahman has composed a beautiful and subtle tune. It starts with this line:

> Sun mere humdum
> *Listen, O companion of mine*

Before we go any further, please can you tell me how you decide which term of endearment to use? Here we have 'humdum', but it could have been 'mere pia' or something else.

G: That's a good question.

There are two considerations. First of all, the words should match the language of the film. There is a family or fabric of words in a film and the song words must fit.

Then there is the tune. If you have a beat—'hum-dum' [*says it with deliberate emphasis on the second syllable—the 'm' sound in dum*], *dum* falls on the beat, it will sound much better than saying 'O saathi re.' The tune gives you a sound and rhythm when you're finding the words.

NMK: Are there some terms of endearment that are now dated?

G: I had an argument once with Rahman over this and I refused to use the word 'sanam' [beloved]. In one of his tunes 'sanam' was used as a dummy word and he liked it very much. I resisted:

'Come what may, I will never use "sanam."'

Rahman was in America and our conversation was taking place on Skype.

'Why? Is "sanam" a bad word?'

'It's a cliché of a cliché!'

'So what? It sounds nice, Gulzar saab.'

'No, I will not use it. I have never used it anywhere. It's such a cliché—stale as rotting vegetables.'

NMK: I see you feel very strongly about the word. What about terms like 'balma' or 'baalam'?

G: If you're writing a folk song or a song for a film set in a village from an earlier era then you could use these terms of endearment. But you would not use them in a modern context. I avoid dated words and there's no point using clichés.

NMK: Coming back to 'Ae hairat-e aashiqui,' we have many options here. It could be 'wondrous love' or 'surprising' love?

G: Not 'wondrous', not 'surprising' love. 'O wonder of love, don't wake me up. Don't let my feet touch the ground…' I am on cloud nine because I am in love. [*both laugh*]

NMK: The line 'don't let my feet touch the ground' is a bit like 'love sweeps me off my feet' in English, right? 'Hairat-e aashiqui' are beautiful words.

G: The coinage is new though 'hairat' and 'aashiqui' are classical Urdu words. I put them together by adding 'e.' This kind of joining of words is common in Persian. You will find many similar words in qawalis, and 'Ae hairat-e aashiqui' has the feel of a qawaali. The tune and the song is somewhat like a qawaali.

NMK: Is this formation of words 'Hairat-e aashiqui' a bit like 'Shaam-e gham ki qasm'?

G: You have found the right example.

NMK: What about 'Kyun Urdu Farsi bolte ho? Dus kehete ho, do ttolte ho'. That's an interesting line.

G: This is meant to be a sort of playful teasing. When she asks her lover why does he speak Urdu or Farsi, she is referring to the words 'hairat-e aashiqui'—so she implies that he should talk in simple language.

'Dus kehete ho, do ttolte ho…' You use ten words when you mean two! Use the word 'mean' here.

NMK: The line suggests he's a lover who exaggerates. A big talker. This characteristic is suggested again in the line 'Jhootton ke shahenshah, bolo na.'

How do I know when 'bolo na' means 'speak up', and when it means 'don't talk'?

G: You're reading the words. You're not hearing them. The tone will tell you whether it's 'speak up' or 'don't talk.'

NMK: You mean the tone of the singer clarifies which it is? To me this is a very important clue in understanding the intention behind song lines.

(Hariharan)
Humesha ishq mein hi jeena
Live forever in love

Ae hairat-e aashiqui jagaa mat
O wonder of love, don't wake me up

Pairon se zameen zameen lagaa mat
Don't let my feet touch the ground

Ae hairat-e aashiqui…

(Alka Yagnik)
Kyun Urdu Farsi bolte ho
Why do you speak Urdu and Farsi?

Dus kehete ho do ttolte ho
You say ten words and mean two

Jhootton ke shahenshah, bolo na
O king of liars, don't talk

(Hariharan)
Kabhi jhaanko meri aankhein
Just look into my eyes

Sunaayein ik daastaan jo hontton se kholona
They tell a story that lips cannot say

Do chaar maheen se lamhon mein
In a few fleeting moments

Umron ke hisaab bhi hote hain
They tell the story of a lifetime

(Alka Yagnik)
Jinhen dekha nahin kal tak kahin bhi
The one who was never seen before…

Ab kokh mein voh chehre bote hain
… is now forming a face in my womb

NMK: Many translators on the Net have confused 'maheen' with 'mahina,' meaning 'months.'

G: The word 'maheen' is Persian and relates to the moon. In Farsi, the word for moon is 'mah.' 'Mahnoor' is moonlight. 'Maheen' also means slight, fine or thin. It has nothing to do with 'months.'

NMK: There are so many songs of yours. Is it possible to have a favourite?

G: It's impossible. I may like a song that works for a particular situation and later prefer another for a different situation. The choice reflects the experience of the moment. There is no numbering involved—this is number one and that is not.

Even in life, you will think of a couplet that describes the immediate situation you're in, or reflects your mindset at that moment.

NMK: What must you bear in mind when writing a song that works like a conversation between a boy and girl? Bearing in mind that unlike English, Hindi and Urdu have a gender system.

G: You give the director a song knowing that this line is for the girl and that line is for the boy. Suddenly the director tells you, supposing the girl sings this line instead? How will the boy reply? So the gender of the words has to change—the thought may remain the same. 'Main kehta hoon' instead of 'Main kehti hoon.'

The little cleverness we lyricists do is worth noting. We say 'Hum kehte hain…' This way you don't commit because you can use 'hum' for boy or girl. So we avoid being specific, in case the directors change the point of view of a verse when they film the song. Hindi provides you with this option.

NMK: I think lyricists today have a big disadvantage because many film characters do not look right when expressing themselves in song. And lip-sync songs look out of place in the more realist stories of current Hindi films. Lyrics aren't as close to the narrative as they once were.

G: That is why most songs play in the background and the hero and heroine do not lip-sync the words. Your observation is absolutely correct.

NMK: What's more, Hindi films seem increasingly to rely on a narrator's voice-over. It provides information, creates narrative bridges, explains the context, eliminates explanatory scenes and sometimes even tells you the emotional state of the characters.

But if we believe the song is the emotional expression of the character, then the voice-over is doing the job of the song. I feel the use of the narrator's voice is a primary reason that the song is becoming redundant in Indian cinema. What we are left with are these big dance numbers that are useful to publicize the release of the film and which end up underscoring the end roller.

G: You're right. It is the narrator that articulates the character's inner expression now. But you have to go with the times.

NMK: I agree. Though I believe songs and the use of music make Indian cinema unique—they are the glue that keeps us attached to Hindi films.

To conclude this fascinating discussion, which could go on for days, I was thinking it would be most interesting to talk about metre and rhythm through your song 'Tujhse naaraaz nahin zindagi'. This lovely song is a RD Burman composition from the 1983 film *Masoom*.

I wonder what other words could have worked on the same metre.

G [*pausing and counting*]: 'Tujh-se naar-aaz nahin zind-agi hai-raan hoon main.' Now this is the metre—you count it. How many beats? Eleven. On the same metre you could have had 'Jeena dushwaar hai zindagi aasaan nahin hai' [Living is difficult, life is not easy].

NMK: Did you give RD Burman the words first or did you write on the tune?

G: I had written the first couplet, which gave Shekhar Kapur the film's title, *Masoom*: 'Tere masoom sawaalon se ...' Then the other couplets were written on the tune.

When Pancham composed the tune, Shekhar suggested we use a new singer from Calcutta, Anup Ghoshal. Pancham immediately agreed. He was always game to try new talent, though he did ask Anup Ghoshal to practice for some days. Diction and delivery is very important—the voice is not everything. You must learn how to render a song.

NMK: Did it take you a long time to write it?

G: It took time because Shekhar and I discussed the scenes in which it would feature. The song is repeated in different parts of the film, not only in one scene. So the couplets were changed to match the narrative.

NMK: For those unfamiliar with the film *Masoom,* it tells the story of an illegitimate young boy, Rahul, beautifully played by Jugal Hansraj, whose mother has died. Rahul is forced to go and live with his father whom he has never met. The father, played by Naseeruddin Shah, has married and the young boy has to find a way of being accepted into his new family.

'Tujhse naaraaz nahin zindagi' seems to alternate between questioning life—a philosophical dialogue—and addressing Rahul. The line 'Zindagi tere gham ne humein rishte naye samjhaaye' describes the boy Rahul's situation. While the line 'tere maasoom sawaalon se pareshaan hoon main' is the father talking to Rahul, and describes his uneasy feelings towards a son he does not really know, and for whom he has no answers.

'Hairaan' could be translated as 'taken aback,' 'perplexed' or 'bewildered.'

G: 'Bewildered' is very good. For 'pareshaan' go with 'puzzle.'

> Tujhse naaraaz nahin zindagi hairaan hoon main
> *Life, I am not angry with you, only bewildered*

> Tere maasoom sawaalon se pareshaan hoon main
> *Your innocent questions puzzle me*

> Jeene ke liye socha hi nahin dard sambhaalne honge
> *Never imagined living would mean embracing sorrow*

> Muskuraayein toh muskuraane ke karz utaarne honge
> *Never thought I'd have to pay for smiling*

> Muskuraaoon kabhi toh lagtaa hai
> jaise hontton pe karz rakha hai
> *If I smile now I wonder if it's inviting another debt*

> Zindagi tere gham ne humein rishte naye samjhaaye
> *Life's sorrows made me understand new relationships*

> Mile jo humein dhoop mein mile chhaaon ke tthande saaye
> *When I found shade, it was under the burning sun*

> Aaj agar bhar aayi hain boondein baras jaayegi
> *If I let my tears fall today they will overflow…*

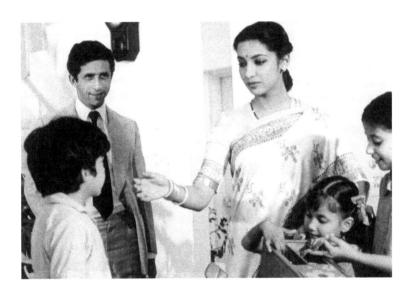

(From left to right) Jugal Hansraj, Naseeruddin Shah, Shabana Azmi, Aradhana Srivastav and Urmila Matondkar in Shekhar Kapur's *Masoom* (1983).

Kal kya pata inke liye aankhein taras jaayengi
... *perhaps tomorrow these eyes of mine*
will long for that single teardrop

Jaane kab goom hua kahaan khoya
ek aansoo chhupa ke rakhaa tha
Who knows where the tear I hid
has vanished

NMK: The song is all about the dilemmas we face in life. The melody is unforgettable too. The words and thoughts are so unusual. You have written amazingly beautiful lines.

G: I am happy that after all these years I am getting this appreciation from you. [*both laugh*]

Maybe that's why you want to write a book on my songs.

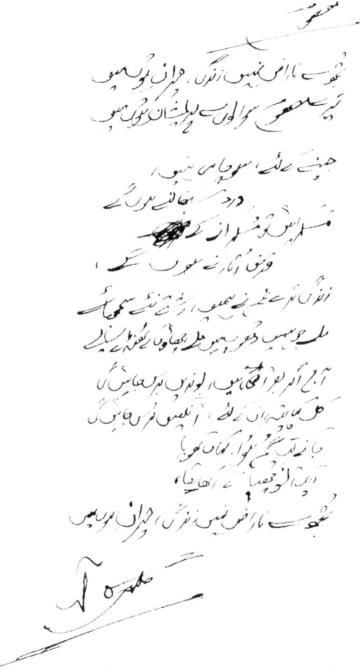

The lyrics of 'Tujhse naaraaz nahin zindagi' in Gulzar's own hand.

Acknowledgements

With thanks to Ravi Singh, Farhana Mahmood, Shonali Gajwani, Justin Chubb, Yashasvi Vachhani, Meghna Gulzar, Priya Kumar, Shameem Kabir, Rudradeep Bhattacharjee, Mani Ratnam and Salim Arif.

Index

Printed in the USA
CPSIA information can be obtained
at www.ICGtesting.com
LVHW020923011124
795360LV00006B/1352